Building Grammar

Grades 1-2

by
Cynthia Salisbury

Published by Instructional Fair
an imprint of
Frank Schaffer Publications®

Instructional Fair

Author: Cynthia Salisbury
Editor: Sara Bierling
Cover Artist: Matthew Van Zomeren

Frank Schaffer Publications®

Instructional Fair is an imprint of Frank Schaffer Publications.

Send all inquiries to:
Frank Schaffer Publications
3195 Wilson Drive NW
Grand Rapids, Michigan 49534

Building Grammar—grades 1-2

ISBN: 1-56822-908-9

6 7 8 9 10 11 12 MAZ 10 09 08 07 06 05

Table of Contents

1-56822-908-9 *Building Grammar*

Who's First in Line?

Write the correct name on each line. The first letter has been written for you. When you are done, the names will be in **alphabetical order**. Three names are done already.

A _____ B _____ C _____ Dustin _____

E _____ F _____ G _____ H _____

I _____ J _____ K _____ L _____

M _____ N _____ O _____ P _____

Quincy _____ R _____ Shelley _____ T _____

U _____ V _____ W _____ X _____

Y _____ Z _____

Jessica	Larry	Karen	Faith	Gloria
Zoe	Holly	~~Dustin~~	Ursula	Patty
Carrie	Manuel	Nancy	Bobby	~~Shelly~~
Wendy	Ian	Xavier	Oliver	~~Quincy~~
Tony	Richie	Angela	Edward	Victor
Yolanda				

Name _____

Which Comes First?

Circle the first letter of each word. Then, write the words in each box in alphabetical order.

apple	map	girl
chair	leaf	book
1. _____	1. _____	1. _____
2. _____	2. _____	2. _____
sun	hand	dog
ring	cloud	radio
1. _____	1. _____	1. _____
2. _____	2. _____	2. _____

1-56822-908-9 *Building Grammar*

Name _____

Putting the Books Back

> When the first letter of two words is the same, you need to use the second letter of the words to decide which word comes first.
>
> Which book comes first?
>   *Black Beauty* or *Brown Bear*
>
> Think: 1. Both names start with **B**.
>   2. The second letter in *Black Beauty* is **l**.
>   3. The second letter in *Brown Bear* is **r**.
>   4. **l** comes before **r** in alphabetical order, so
>   *Black Beauty* comes before *Brown Bear*.

Use the numbers 1–12 to show the alphabetical order of these books. You may need to use scratch paper to figure it out.

_____ One Fine Day

_____ Snakes are Nothing to Sneeze At

_____ Charlotte's Web

_____ Don't Touch

_____ Pickle Juice

_____ Cloudy with a Chance of Meatballs

_____ Nate the Great

_____ Sylvester and the Magic Pebble

_____ Fox in Socks

_____ No Such Things

_____ Dinosaur Time

_____ Owls in the Family

Try This Alphabetize your classroom library or your books at home.

1-56822-908-9 *Building Grammar*

Name _____

Nouns Name Things

A **noun** is a word that names a thing.
paper, crayon

Write the correct noun for each object under its picture. You may use the Word Bank for help.

1. _____

2. _____

3. _____

4. _____

5. _____

6. _____

Word Bank		
desk	pillow	chair
glass	book	pencil

1-56822-908-9 *Building Grammar*

Name _____

Writing the Naming Part

Nouns name people, places, and things.

the boy = person
the supermarket = place
a tent = thing

Write one of the nouns from the fort on each line to begin each sentence.

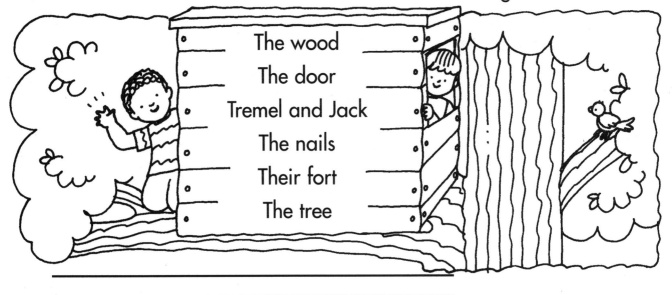

The wood
The door
Tremel and Jack
The nails
Their fort
The tree

1. _____ built a fort.

2. _____ was very tall.

3. _____ was easy to find.

4. _____ were rusted and bent.

5. _____ had a window.

6. _____ was crooked.

Name _____

Munchin' on Lunch

> **Nouns** name people, places, and things.
>
> *boy, teacher = people*
> *playground, classroom = places*
> *jump rope, lunch bag = things*

Circle all the nouns below. Draw a line from each noun that could go in your lunch to the bag.

napkin   milk

apple   hill

hot   cookie

carrots   clouds

red   cheese

cracker   Dad

Name _____

Aimee's Day

> **Nouns** can name people, places, and things.
>
> Aimee = person
> school = place
> chips = thing

Circle all the nouns in the sentences below.

Aimee goes to the zoo to watch Ruby, the elephant, paint pictures.

Aimee and John enjoy ice-cream cones.

Aimee and her grandfather take a long walk by the lake.

Aimee and her sister ride bikes to the park.

Write each different noun you circled under the correct category.

Person	Place	Thing
_____	_____	_____
_____	_____	_____
_____	_____	_____
_____	_____	_____
_____	_____	_____

1-56822-908-9 *Building Grammar*

Name _____

Let's Go on a Nature Hike!

> **Nouns** name people, places, or things.
>
> *Rachel = person*
> *trail = place*
> *rock = thing*

Find the nouns in the wordsearch that might be seen on a nature hike.
Oops! There are some words in the bank that aren't nouns. Cross those
out first.

Word Bank

bubbly	leaves	rode	pine tree
pinecones	minnows	owl	mountain
gigantic	fluffy	fast	waterfall
squirrels	hiker	stream	warm

w	x	z	a	p	i	n	e	t	r	e	e
a	s	q	u	i	r	r	e	l	s	m	j
t	v	w	x	n	y	z	q	e	o	o	l
e	h	i	k	e	r	p	r	a	l	u	q
r	s	t	u	c	c	d	f	v	r	n	t
f	a	m	r	o	w	l	g	e	b	t	v
a	n	m	i	n	n	o	w	s	e	a	y
l	o	s	u	e	b	e	h	i	a	i	r
l	w	x	p	s	t	r	e	a	m	n	k

Name _____

One Pencil, Two Erasers

Many nouns for people, places, and things add **s** to the end to show more than one. These are called **plural nouns**.

I have one pencil, two erasers, and ten crayons.

Pete and Sara are cleaning their desks. Help them make a list of the school tools they have. Remember to add an **s** when there is more than one. Write the number and the name of the tool on the lines.

_____ _____

_____ _____

_____ _____

_____ _____

_____ _____ _____ _____

_____ _____

Name _____

Knock! Knock!

> To make a word that names more than one person, place, or thing, you sometimes add **s** to the end. This is called a **plural noun**.
>
> boy | girl
> plural = boy**s** | plural = girl**s**

Write down who has come to your door. Remember to add an **s** when there is more than one. Use the Word Bank for help. The first one has been done for you.

Knock! Knock!

Who's There?

1. Two boys on <u>bicycles</u> are here.

2. Mary brought a cage with six

   _____ .

3. Two _____ are riding their skateboards.

4. A lady has nine _____ for the party.

5. Uh! Oh! These _____ came to the wrong party.

Word Bank

balloon	clown	dog
bird	~~bicycle~~	

Name _____

Jobs Galore

A **plural noun** names more than one person, place, or thing. When a noun ends in a consonant followed by the letter *y*, change the final *y* to *i* and add **es**.

story = stor**ies**   sky = sk**ies**   penny = penn**ies**

The kids at Pleasant School thought of some ideas to raise money. Write the plural form of the correct noun on each line. The Word Bank will help you.

1. Ben and Maria had three pizza _____.

2. On Saturday, Mrs. Alton's class took care of _____.

3. The students brought in their extra _____.

4. The fifth-grade students read _____ for fifty cents each.

5. School _____ donated money from yard sales.

6. Other _____ gave extra books.

Word Bank

party	baby	library
story	family	penny

1-56822-908-9 *Building Grammar*

Name _____

Where Are My Things?

To make some nouns **plural**, we add **es**. We add **es** to nouns that end with these letters:

s as in grass (grasses)   *sh as in dish (dishes)*
x as in box (boxes)   *ch as in lunch (lunches)*

To find out where forgetful Frank put his school supplies, write the plural ending (**s** or **es**) of each word on the line. Then find the words in the wordsearch.

He put his **glass** _____

in one of his **pocket** _____.

He left his **pencil** _____

and two of his **book** _____

at the reading table. He put the

book about **fox** _____

on the **box** _____ in the

library. When the bell rang, he

carried the box with all the

lunch _____ for all the

children in both second grade

class _____ to the

tree _____ on the

playground.

z	e	f	t	g	f	l	b	p	f
a	d	o	r	c	i	u	g	r	y
b	o	x	e	s	s	n	l	t	p
l	i	e	e	j	k	c	a	v	e
u	k	s	s	l	e	h	s	w	n
m	c	l	a	s	s	e	s	s	c
h	p	s	m	q	o	s	e	n	i
o	n	d	b	o	o	k	s	x	l
s	r	q	p	o	c	k	e	t	s

Name _____

Don't Step on My Feet

> Some tricky nouns change in the middle to make them **plural**.
>
>   one *foot*, two *feet*
>
>   one *goose*, two *geese*

See if you can find the tricky plural for each of the nouns below. Use the answers to fill in the crossword puzzle.

Across

2. A sign posted on the fence said: No _____ (**child**) beyond this point.

3. Mr. Wood had 50 _____ (**man**) working on the library building.

5. Is your foot on my _____ (**foot**)?

7. There are also four _____ (**woman**) on the crew.

Down

1. About 30 _____ (**mouse**) scurried out.

4. Many _____ (**person**) came to the dedication.

6. Did you lose your front _____ (**tooth**)?

1-56822-908-9 *Building Grammar*

Name _____

That's Mine

Add **'s** to the end of a word to show that something belongs to someone. This is called a **possessive noun**.

Carol's cat is small.

Underline the possessive noun in each sentence. Draw a line to match each sentence with the correct picture.

1. Janie's hair is curly.

2. That wagon is Jacob's.

3. The bike's tire is flat.

4. The dog's ears are floppy.

5. That is the kitten's ball.

Try This Write down the names of objects in your classroom. Now write sentences that tell to whom the objects belong. Make sure to use possessive nouns.

17

Name _____

Whose?

Add **'s** (apostrophe + s) to the end of a word to show that something belongs to someone. This is called a **possessive noun**.
That bike belongs to Sandy.
That is Sandy's bike.

Write the correct noun in each blank.

_____ p.j.'s are red.

Marta   Martas   Marta's

This is _____ toothbrush.

Joels   Joel   Joel's

My _____ ball is missing.

brother's   brothers   brother

That _____ dress is pretty.

girl   girl's   girls

The _____ bell is broken.

schools   school's   school

This is the _____ bone.

dog's   dog   dogs

The _____ teacher is Ms. Popp.

class   classes   class's

The _____ fur is soft.

bear   bear's   bears

1-56822-908-9 *Building Grammar*

Name _____

Breakfast at the Creature Café

> **Nouns** name people, places, or things.
> *A **lizard** with one **eye** is on the **wall**.*
> **Verbs** tell what someone or something is doing.
> *A lizard **climbs** the wall.*

Read each sentence. Underline the nouns. Read each sentence again. Circle the verbs.

1. Lizards leap onto our table.

2. Monkeys swing down for bananas.

3. Giraffes stretch their necks and nibble some leaves.

4. Wart hogs slurp their oatmeal.

5. The goats lick our plates clean.

6. A chimp rings up our bill.

Try This   Write a story about a crazy breakfast.

19

Name _____

Rockin' at Recess

> **Verbs** show action.
>
> *I **run** to school everyday.*
> *Josh **hides** in the bushes.*

Look for the following action words in the wordsearch below: **jump**, **swing**, **climb**, **hide**, **run**, **catch**, and **leap**. The picture clues around the wordsearch will help you find the words.

c	a	t	c	h	j	d
t	h	r	l	k	u	e
x	y	c	i	s	m	r
r	u	n	m	w	p	l
m	f	j	b	i	m	e
x	a	q	b	n	w	a
h	i	d	e	g	y	p

Try This   Draw a picture. See how many verbs (action words) you can draw.

1-56822-908-9 *Building Grammar*

Name _____

Animal Action

> **Verbs** tell us what is happening in a sentence. Some verbs show lots of action:
> *walk, run, jump, hop, eat, swing, pick, fly, climb*
> Other verbs tell about things we do:
> *look, talk, read, hear, think, live*

Write in the missing verb in each sentence below. You can find all the verbs you will need in the examples at the top of the page.

1. Can rabbits _____ higher than kangaroos?

2. Can elephants _____ up peanuts with their trunks?

3. Do monkeys _____ from tree to tree using their tails?

4. Can a lion _____ a tree?

5. How far can a hummingbird _____ each day?

6. Could a penguin _____ in the desert?

7. When can you _____ a coyote howling?

8. What doctor could _____ to the animals?

Name _____

Animals Move

> **Verbs** show the action in a sentence. Verbs tell what someone or something does.
>
> *Tamara **ran** out of school.*

Read each sentence and underline the verbs. Then find each verb in the wordsearch. **Hint:** There are twelve different verbs in the wordsearch.

Monkeys swing from tree to tree.

An alligator swims in the swamp.

Tarantulas crawl across rocks and sand.

Some snakes can slither up trees.

Other snakes wriggle in water.

Some kangaroos can hop more than 25 feet!

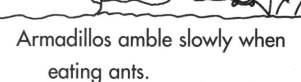

s	l	u	r	p	g	f	s
t	v	m	e	w	c	d	l
p	s	c	u	r	r	y	e
h	l	b	g	i	a	t	e
s	w	i	n	g	w	h	p
w	p	o	p	g	l	o	s
i	a	m	b	l	e	v	h
m	x	a	v	e	u	e	o
s	l	i	t	h	e	r	p

Armadillos amble slowly when eating ants.

Prairie dogs pop out of their holes and scurry around for food.

Grizzly bears sleep in their caves all winter.

Hummingbirds hover like helicopters and slurp nectar from flowers.

1-56822-908-9 *Building Grammar*

Name _____

Saving the Planet

Add **s** to a verb that tells what one person, animal, or thing does.

*The boy **helps** the earth by recycling.*

Do not add **s** to verbs to tell what two or more people, animals, or things do.

*The boys **help** the earth by recycling.*

Copy the correct verb (a. or b.) for each sentence onto the writing lines.

_____ a. collect   b. collects _____

1. Many kids _____ aluminum cans.

_____ a. wants   b. want _____

2. The girl _____ to recycle them.

_____ a. save   b. saves _____

3. Boys and girls _____ newspapers.

_____ a. bring   b. brings _____

4. Jack _____ old magazines to be recycled.

_____ a. gathers   b. gather _____

5. Some boys _____ old telephone books.

1-56822-908-9 *Building Grammar*

Name _____

1, 2, 3 Strikes You're Out!

> A verb must agree in number with the subject of the sentence. If the subject of the sentence is one, add an **s** to the verb.
>
> *She plays with Ryan.*
>
> If the subject of the sentence is more than one, the verb does not need an **s**.
>
> *They play with Ryan.*

Read each sentence out loud. Ask yourself if the sentence has one or more than one. Underline the correct verb and write it on the line.

1. The first batter _____ (run, runs) to first base.

2. The next batter _____ (swings, swing) at a low ball.

3. The right fielder _____ (drop, drops) the ball.

4. The batter _____ (score, scores) a run.

5. The pitcher _____ (walk, walks) three Cubs.

6. The next two players _____ (strike, strikes) out.

7. The last Cub _____ (hit, hits) a home run.

8. The Cubs on all four bases _____ (score, scores).

Name _____

Library Help

> The ending of a verb tells whether it is in present or past tense. **Present tense** is what's happening now.
>
> *I **pack** books in boxes.*
>
> **Past tense** is what happened in the past.
>
> *I **packed** books in boxes yesterday.*

Write the correct verb in each sentence.

1. Last week Mrs. Poppins _____ the library.
   (tours, toured)

2. Yesterday, I _____ Mrs. Alden stack books.
   (help, helped)

3. I love to _____ stories.
   (write, wrote)

4. The janitor _____ the floor yesterday.
   (washes, washed)

5. José _____ books on the shelf today.
   (puts, put)

6. Amelia _____ the tables just a few minutes ago.
   (cleans, cleaned)

7. The bulldozers _____ the school this morning.
   (leave, left)

8. I _____ in a bean-bag chair and watch.
   (sit, sat)

Name _____

Yesterday We Played

Some verbs add **ed** to the end to tell about action that happened in the past. These are called **past tense verbs**.

Today I play with Angela.
*Yesterday I play**ed** with Sam.*

Fill in this journal entry with verbs from the Word Bank below.

← mom

sister ↓ Ha-Ha

Word Bank

bicycled   rolled   laughed
fished   wanted   giggled
               looked

Monday, August 14

Julie's Journal

   Yesterday my family and I _____ to the park. Mom made fried chicken, a green salad, and rolls. After eating, my Dad and I _____ in the lake. My little sister _____ down the hill. She _____ and _____ . At three o'clock we _____ dessert. We got on our bikes and _____ for an ice-cream shop. What do you think my favorite flavor is?

Name _____

Guess What We Did

> Many action words that tell what happened in the past tense end in **ed**.
>
> *Bob and Mary **visit** their friend.*
> *Yesterday, Bob and Mary **visited** their friend.*

Read what each group of kids did yesterday during lunch. Underline the past tense verbs that end in **ed** in each story. The group with the most verbs in the past tense (**ed**) did the safest thing.

Group 1

At recess we played on the playground. Mrs. Alton's cell phone buzzed. She waved her hands. Everyone stopped playing.

Mrs. Alton yelled, "Fire!"

We noticed the fire was in the garbage can. We walked to the hose and turned it on. Before the firemen arrived, we put out the fire. The bell rang. We went back to class.

Group 2

At lunch, we started walking to the cafeteria. Suddenly, Mrs. Alton yelled, "Fire!"

The fire truck sirens screamed. The men shouted to each other. They unrolled the hoses. They turned on the water. The firemen sprayed the garbage can. The fire was put out. We walked to the cafeteria. We gobbled our food and walked to recess.

Which group has the most action words in past tense (ed)?

Group #:_____

1-56822-908-9 *Building Grammar*

Name _____

I'm Gonna . . .

> To talk about what is going to happen later, put a special verb, called a **helping verb**, in front of the regular verb. The helping verb used to talk about the future is **will**.
>
> I walk home. (now)
> I **will walk** home. (later)

Change the sentences below so they say what is going to happen later. The first one is done for you.

1. **NOW:** I eat apples.

   LATER: <u>I **will eat** apples. _____</u>

2. **NOW:** Mary rides her bike.

   LATER: _____

3. **NOW:** Josh loves chocolate.

   LATER: _____

4. **NOW:** The baby cries.

   LATER: _____

5. **NOW:** I jump rope.

   LATER: _____

Name _____

The Zoo Album

> **Linking verbs** link the first part of a sentence to the last part. They do not show action.
>
> *The wolf **is** in the largest cage.*
> *Three wolves **are** in the largest cage.*
> *I **am** afraid of wolves.*

Underline the linking verb in each sentence.

1. The giant tortoise is green with brown and green spots.

2. The alligators are smaller than the giant tortoises.

3. The hippo and giraffe are next to each other.

4. This zebra is friendly.

5. I am the zookeeper at Park Zoo.

6. I am also the head tour guide.

7. Park Zoo is very large.

8. Harmony Farm is a great attraction at the zoo.

29

Name _____

Jump, Hop, and Run

> **Linking verbs** link the first part of a sentence to the last part. They do not show action.
>
> *The giraffe **is** the tallest animal at Park Zoo.*
> *The turtles **are** the slowest animals at the zoo.*

Read each sentence to yourself. Write the correct linking verb in each sentence. If the subject is singular (one), use **is**. If the subject is plural (more than one), use **are**.

1. The wolf _____ in the cage next to the coyote.

2. The polar bears and the penguins _____ in a new part of Park Zoo called Winter Express.

3. Owls and bats _____ some of the nighttime animals at the zoo.

4. The zebra _____ the animal that looks like a horse with stripes.

5. The monkeys _____ the funniest animals at Park Zoo.

1-56822-908-9 *Building Grammar*

Name _____

Stop! Halt! Whoa!

> **Synonyms** are words that mean almost the same thing.
> the **scary** tiger = the **frightening** tiger
> the **nice** zookeeper = the **pleasant** zookeeper

Use the Word Bank to find new words that mean almost the same thing as the underlined words. Write them on the lines.

Lions have a loud <u>growl</u>. _____

You can see the monkeys <u>sway</u> from tree to tree. _____

Giraffes <u>select</u> leaves from tall trees. _____

Listen! Wolves <u>wail</u> at night. _____

Careful! A snake may <u>slide</u> into your lunch. _____

Word Bank

choose   slither   swing   howl   roar

Name _____

Like Another

> **Synonyms** are different words that mean almost the same thing.
>
> *Huge* is another way to say **big**.

Fill in the crossword puzzle with words that mean the same as the underlined words in the sentences. Use the Word Bank for help.

Across

5. Matt is going to <u>guide</u> us to the gym.
6. Our teacher bakes <u>wonderful</u> treats.
8. That was the <u>final</u> question on the spelling test.

Down

1. I play tag with my <u>pals</u>.
2. I will <u>give</u> some of my chips to Cate.
3. I like books with <u>happy</u> endings.
4. It is very <u>dreary</u> outside today.
7. My sister is the <u>smallest</u> student in third grade.

Word Bank

friends	gloomy
lead	offer
last	marvelous
shortest	cheerful

1-56822-908-9 *Building Grammar*

Name _____

Outside In, Inside Out

Antonyms are words that mean the opposite of each other.

Inside is the opposite of **outside**.

Circle each word that is the opposite of each picture.

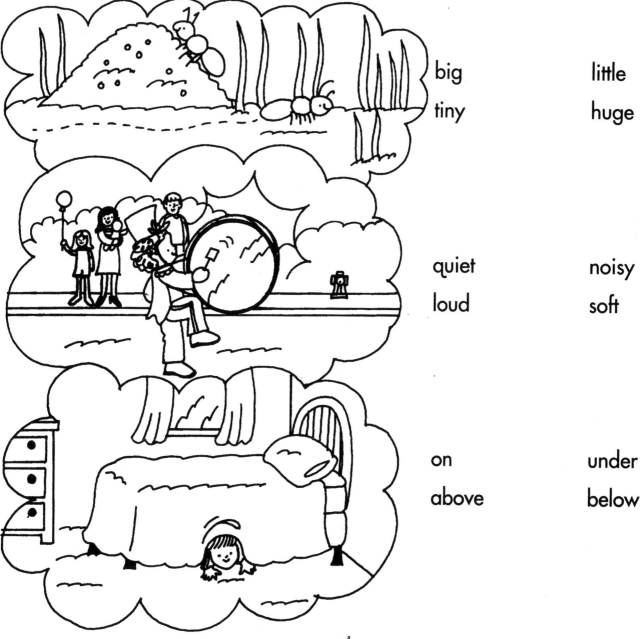

big   little

tiny   huge

quiet   noisy

loud   soft

on   under

above   below

1-56822-908-9 *Building Grammar*

Name _____

The Turtle n' the Hare

> **Antonyms** are words that mean the opposite of each other.
>
> *Hot* is the opposite of *cold*.

Look at each picture. Draw a line to the sentence that is the opposite.

Giraffes have <u>long</u> necks so they can eat leaves in <u>tall</u> trees.

Ellie the Elephant has <u>big</u> ears.

Polar bears have <u>white</u> fur to look like snow.

A jackrabbit's ears are very <u>thin</u> and <u>long</u>.

Try This Describe some students in your class using these opposite words: tall or short, curly hair or straight hair, funny or serious, happy or sad, and so on.

1-56822-908-9 *Building Grammar*

Name _____

I Rode on a Road

> **Homophones** are words that sound alike but are spelled differently and have different meanings.
>
> **Ate** means to eat yesterday.
> **Eight** is a number that tells how many.

Match the pictures and words that sound the same by drawing a line.

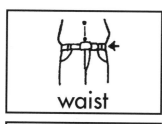

waist

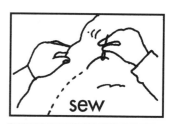

sew

pair

rain

rein

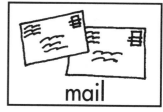

mail

sow

waste

male

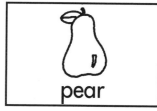

pear

Try This Write a story using all the homophones from above.

1-56822-908-9 *Building Grammar*

Name _____

What We Ate at Eight

> **Homophones** are words that sound alike but are spelled differently and have different meanings.
>
> **See** means to look at something.
> **Sea** means the same as ocean.

Find the correct word to use in each part of the sentence. Then write it on the line.

1. _____ of us went to Burger-matic where we _____ hamburgers and French fries. (**eight, ate**)

2. The bus _____ for the ride to the county _____ was 50¢. (**fair, fare**)

3. Your _____ _____ what we will have for dinner. (**knows, nose**)

4. The doctor said my _____ will _____ faster if I keep it uncovered. (**heel, heal**)

5. Did you _____ the invitation with your left or

   _____ hand? (**right, write**)

6. _____ notice you have one blue and one brown

   _____ . (**I, eye**)

Try This   Write a story using the homophones above.

1-56822-908-9 *Building Grammar*

Name _____

To, Two, Too, or TuTu

> **To**, **two**, and **too** are words we use a lot. Each one has a different meaning.
>
> **To** is a word used in front of a verb.
>   *I like **to** camp.*
>
> **Two** is a number word.
>   *I have **two** candy bars in my sleeping bag.*
>
> **Too** means *more than enough*, and is also used to mean *also*.
>   *I had **too** much chocolate.* (more than enough)
>   *My friend is going to the campout, **too**.* (also)

Write the correct **to**, **two**, or **too** in the blanks to finish these sentences.

1. Before you go _____ sleep, brush your teeth.

2. I'm hungry. I want _____ more candy bars.

3. Uh! Oh! I'm _____ big for this chair.

4. I need _____ buy some marshmallows for the campout.

5. Help me! This box is _____ heavy for one person to carry.

6. We need _____ carry the box to the backyard.

7. Look! Katy is _____ short to reach the latch on the gate.

8. Get a ladder _____ stand on.

9. I'll need the ladder, _____ .

Name _____

Marshmallow Roast

Homophones are words that sound the same but are spelled differently and have different meanings.

I **hear** something.   hear = to listen to a sound
Stay **here**, and I'll look.   here = a place

Choose the correct homophone for each sentence. You may have to look up the meaning of some words in the dictionary.

When I _____ my invitations, I asked everyone to bring
                (scent, sent)

something _____ our campout. When the _____ sky
            (for, four)   (blew, blue)

turned gray, the clouds covered the _____, but it didn't rain.
                                        (sun, son)

We put bales of _____ around the fire so we could sing
                (hey, hay)

camp songs together. My aunt _____ some special chocolate
                            (sent, scent)

from San Francisco for our s'mores. Mom thought it would be better to

_____ the chocolate. Her idea did not turn out _____.
(grate, great)   (grate, great)

The chocolate melted and fell all over.

The best part of the night was when a _____ walked through
                                    (dough, doe)

the woods with four other _____ .
                        (dear, deer)

Name _____

One Plus One Equals One

Sometimes two words are joined together to make one new word. The new word is called a **compound** word.

cow + boy = cowboy

Look at the words and pictures below. Add the words together and write the new word on the line.

bird + house = _____

horse + shoe = _____

pan + cake = _____

sun + flower = _____

rain + coat = _____

Try This Think of as many compound words as you can. Write down the different parts of each word, just like the ones above.

_____ + _____ = _____

1-56822-908-9 *Building Grammar*

Name _____

Fun on a Zoofari!

> **Compound words** are two words joined together to make a new word.
>
> *foot + ball = football*

Fill in the things we will need for our Zoofari. Use two words from the Word Bank to help you put together a compound word for each sentence.

1. Take a _____ to see where you are walking at night.

2. Buy a _____ and a pencil to write about the animals.

3. Bring _____ seeds to feed the birds.

4. The _____ said it might rain, so let's take an umbrella.

5. We should also pack a _____ .

6. We will buy a train ticket at the _____ office.

7. I will bring some _____ and canteloupe.

8. Could you bring some _____ without any salt?

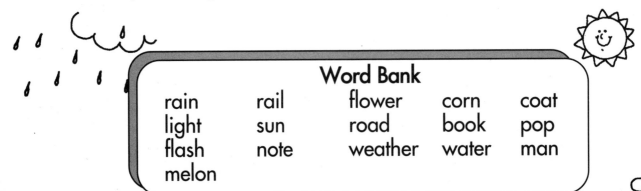

Word Bank

rain	rail	flower	corn	coat
light	sun	road	book	pop
flash	note	weather	water	man
melon				

1-56822-908-9 *Building Grammar*

Name _____

Pow! Ouch! Yikes!

> The **sound** of some words make you
> think of their meaning.
> *swish*
> *buzz*

Draw a line from each sentence to the correct picture.

1. What goes brring-brring?

2. What goes drip-drip?

3. What goes bang-bang?

4. What goes honk-honk?

5. What goes toot-toot?

6. What goes boom-boom?

41

1-56822-908-9 *Building Grammar*

Name _____

Harmony Farm

> The **sound** of some words make you
> think of their meaning.
> > *swish*
> > *buzz*

Look at these pictures from Harmony Farm. Use the Word Bank to write
the correct sound word on the line.

Here! Chick! Chick! Chick!

The ducks in the pond are talking.

Woodpeckers make a
hole in the barn wood.

Up in the trees the
birds are singing.

The pigs want food.

One of the goats ate too much!

Word Bank

| Cheep! | Quack! | Oink! |
| Rat-a-tat-tat! | Hiccup! | Tweet! |

1-56822-908-9 *Building Grammar*

Name _____

More Books, Take a Look

> **Rhyming words** are words that end with the same sound. Say these rhyming words out loud. Can you hear the rhyme?
>
> box   fox   hat   mat
> corn   horn   dog   frog

Circle all the book titles that rhyme. Then write the rhyming words from each title on the line.

1. *Kitten Can* _____

2. *Rat-a-Tat, Pitter-Pat* _____

3. *Hop on Pop* _____

4. *Like Jake and Me* _____

5. *Whose Shoe?* _____

6. *Amelia Bedelia* _____

7. *Hunches in Bunches* _____

8. *Aunt Flossie's Hats* _____

9. *Is Your Mama a Llama?* _____

10. *Sheep in a Jeep* _____

Try This Make up some rhyming book titles of your own.

    1-56822-908-9 *Building Grammar*

Name _____

Should We Play?

> **Rhyming words** are words that end with the same sound. Use your ears to hear the rhyme.
>
> *game, name*
> *rover, over*

Underline the rhyming words in each jump-rope rhyme.
Hint: It helps if you say them out loud.

Red Rover, Red Rover
Turn the jump rope over.
Faster and slower,
Higher and lower,
Let's speed up the game.
I'll shout out a name.

Baby, Baby in the tub,
Mama forgot to put in the plug.
Oh, what a shame!
Oh, what a pain!
There goes Baby down the drain!

Try This Make up a jump rope rhyme of your own. Here are some rhyming words to get started with, or choose your own.

ring	itsy	fox	trip	hat	coat
ding	bitsy	box	slip	sat	boat

44

1-56822-908-9 *Building Grammar*

Name _____

The Midnight Writer

There are lots of **silly words**. Some come from other languages or people's names. Many silly words are just made up.

hoity-toity

Read the mysterious letter Sue found under her pillow. Underline all the silly words. **Hint:** There are 5.

Dear Friend,

When you and your friends were walking helter-skelter in the woods, someone was watching you. Does that give you the heebie-jeebies?

I bet you are thinking, "Who could it be?"

Jeepers-creepers! Do you think someone is looking for you? Or is it just one of your friends watching you?

Whoever or whatever, it left some footprints. Interested? If so, meet me for a chitchat.

A roly-poly friend

P.S. Bring puppy food and a leash.

Can you solve the mystery? Who or what is following Sue?

Try This Look up some other silly words in books or dictionaries or make up some of your own. Write a story or letter using some fun, made-up words.

Name _____

Mathantics

> Numbers can be written many different ways.
> One way is to write a number as a word.
>
> 1 = one   2 = two   3 = three

Find the answers to these problems. Write your answers as words.

1. To ride on a seasaw you need _____ friend.

2. The _____ bears had a visit from Goldilocks.

3. If two friends sit at a table and three more sit down, there will be _____ at the table.

4. The number word that comes after eight and before ten is _____ .

5. A car has _____ wheels.

6. Katie brought 3 pieces of gum. Jennifer brought 4 pieces. How many people can have gum? _____

7. There is only one chair at the table. How many people can sit at the table? _____

8. For our game, we need 2 people to hold the jumprope and 2 people to jump. How many do we need for our game? _____

Try This Use dice to play "Roll and Write." Roll the dice (you may also use one die) and write the numbers as words.

1-56822-908-9 *Building Grammar*

ordinal numbers

Name ______________________

First Place!

Sometimes we need to use special number words to show how people or things are related to each other. If someone won a race you would say:

Danny came in first.

The word ***first*** is called an ordinal number. The ordinal numbers are: **first**, **second**, **third**, **fourth**, **fifth**, **sixth**, **seventh**, **eighth**, **ninth**, and **tenth**.

Look at the picture below. Write the correct ordinal number next to each racer's picture.

1. is ______________________

2. is ______________________

3. is ______________________

4. is ______________________

5. is ______________________

1-56822-908-9 *Building Grammar*

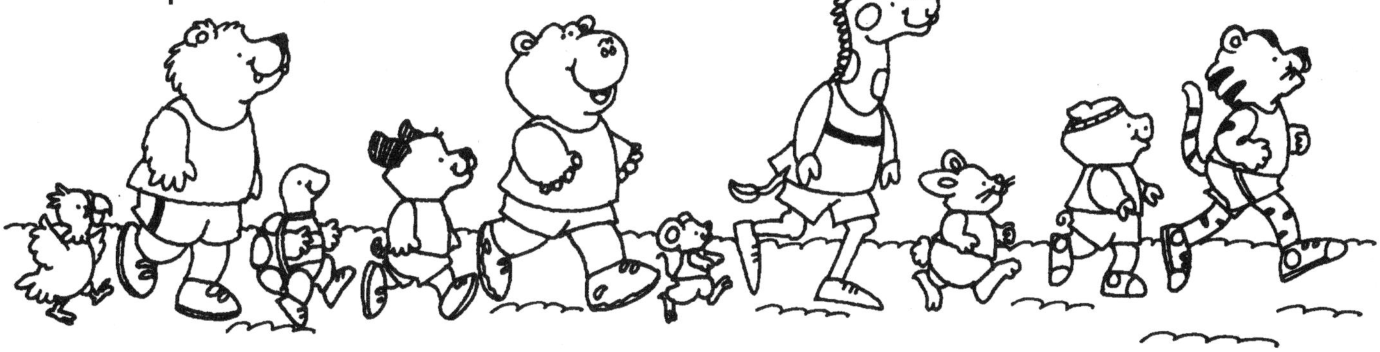

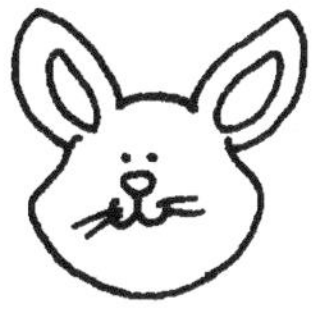

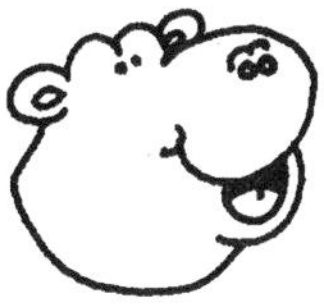

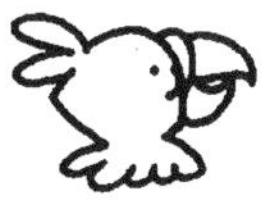

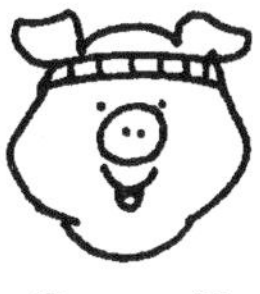

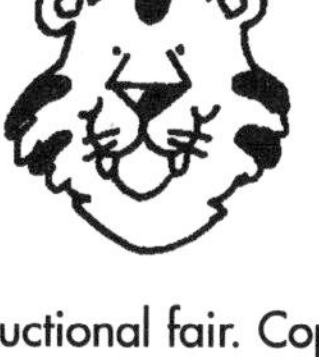

Name _____

Crazy Crayons

> **Color words** help to tell about people, places, and things.
> *Dan is wearing a **purple** hat.*
> *The flag is **red**, **white**, and **blue**.*

Solve these color riddles.

| green   red   white   orange   brown   yellow   blue   black   purple |

The color of the stars on the American flag is _____ .

A chalkboard can be the same color as grass, _____ .

A gingerbread man is _____ .

An apple can be green, yellow, or _____ .

The sun is _____ .

The sky is _____ .

A car has _____ tires.

A plum is red or _____ .

Pumpkins are _____ .

Try This Close your eyes and choose 20 crayons. Open your eyes and write a list of the colors you have in ABC order.

1-56822-908-9 *Building Grammar*

Name _____

Whose Smelly Sneakers?

An **adjective** is a word that describes a noun. Adjectives can tell about nouns by color, number, shape, size, feel, and smell.

The <u>small</u> <u>yellow</u> and <u>white</u> tennis shoes are Mary's.

Color each pair of tennis shoes to match the color word(s) that describes them. Then, underline the word(s) that tells about the shape, size, feel, or smell of each pair.

1. Jimmy's yellow sneakers are very long.

2. Jenny's purple tennis shoes have a square toe.

3. Antonio's red and white striped sneakers have short laces.

4. Yoshi's blue sneakers are too small for her.

5. Missy's green tennis shoes are the smallest ones in our class.

6. These orange sneakers are wet and smelly.

Name _____

This Is My House

> **Adjectives** can tell about things by size, shape, color, or number.
>
> **blue** book   **little** boy
> **three** poodles   **square** box

Help Carl finish these sentences that tell about his house. Use words that describe by color, size, shape, or number.

1. I live in a _____ house. (**color**)

2. It is a _____ house. (**size**)

3. There are _____ windows in my house. (**number**)

4. There are _____ violets and _____

   roses growing in my yard. (**color**)

5. My front door has a _____ window in it. (**shape**)

6. I have a very _____ driveway. (**size**)

7. I have _____ pet(s). (**number**)

8. It is a _____ rabbit. (**color**)

Try This Draw a picture of your house. Put in as many details as you can. Then write some sentences that describe your house.

1-56822-908-9 *Building Grammar*

Name _____

I'm Reading!

Adjectives tell more about nouns.

Robert is a nice boy.   ***Nice** tells more about Robert.*

We go to the school library   ***School** tells about*
on Tuesdays.   *the library.*

I like to read joke and   ***Joke** and **riddle** tell more*
riddle books.   *about books.*

Look at the list of books. Circle the word in each book title that tells more about the person, place, or thing. On the line, write whether the adjective tells more about a **person** or an **animal**, a **place**, or a **thing**.

Silly Sally   _____

Green Eggs and Ham   _____

Little Bear   _____

The Surprise Party   _____

The Snowy Day   _____

Alexander and the Wind-up Mouse _____

Try This   Make up some book titles of your own with words that tell more about people, places, or things.

Name _____

Cloudy or Sunny?

> Some **adjectives** tell what the weather is like today or what it might be like tomorrow.
>
> *Today is cloudy.*

Pretend you are the weather person. Look at the pictures below. Write two adjectives from the Word Bank on the lines next to each picture.

_____

_____

_____

_____

_____

_____

Word Bank

sunny	rainy	cloudy	hot	snowy
sizzling	stormy	gray	warm	icy
windy	foggy	freezing	cold	

Name _____

Who's Faster?

Adjectives that compare two things end in **er**.
It's cold inside.
It is colder outside than inside.

Use the Word Bank to write a comparing word in the blank of each sentence below. Then answer the question with a sentence.

Word Bank

| colder | slower | darker | faster | longer |
| smaller | bigger | taller | warmer | |

1. Which is _____ , Alaska or Hawaii?

   _____

2. What's _____ , night or day?

   _____

3. Is a turtle _____ than a rabbit?

   _____

4. Who is _____ , an ant or an alligator?

   _____

5. Is Africa _____ than the North Pole?

   _____

6. Is your teacher _____ than you?

   _____

Name _____

Who's the Fastest?

> **Adjectives** that compare more than two things end in **est**.
>
> *Their houses are cold, but my house is the coldest.*
> *My bicycle is the largest of all my toys.*

Look at the picture below. Use the Word Bank to complete the sentences with the correct **est** comparing word. Some adjectives won't be used.

Word Bank
tallest   coldest   fastest   biggest   smallest
widest   slowest   kindest   longest

1. The roadrunner is the _____ runner. He won the race.

2. Turtle is the _____ runner. He came in last.

3. With her cage full of ice, the penguin is the _____ racer.

4. Since the jaguar offered to carry the kangaroo, he may be the _____ animal in the race.

5. The anteater is the runner with the _____ nose.

6. The _____ runner is the mouse.

1-56822-908-9 *Building Grammar*

Name _____

Taller, Higher . . .

Adjectives that compare usually end in **er** or **est**. When we compare two people, places, or things, we use **er**.

Tom is taller than Roberto.

When we compare three or more, we add **est**.

Samantha is the tallest of all the girls.

Use the graph and the Word Bank to complete the sentences below.

Jenny   José   Maria   Dan

1. is the _____ .

2.  and are _____ than .

3.  is _____ than .

4. is the _____ .

Word Bank

taller   tallest   shorter   shortest

1-56822-908-9 *Building Grammar*

Name _____

As the Years Go By

> **Adjectives** that compare two people, places, or things usually end in **er**. Adjectives that compare three or more usually end in **est**.
>
> *Paige is faster.*
> *Paige is the fastest.*

Use the graph and the Word Bank to complete the sentences below.

Kyle	☆ ☆ ☆
Ashley	☆ ☆ ⌐
Roberto	☆ ☆ ☆ ☆
Sara	☆ ☆ ☆ ⌐
Mrs. Alton	☆ ☆ ☆ ☆ ☆ ☆ ☆ ☆ ☆ ☆ ☆ ☆ ☆ ☆ ☆

☆ = 2 years

1. Mrs. Alton is the _____ .

2. Ashley is the _____ .

3. Roberto is _____ than Sara.

4. Kyle is _____ than Sara.

Word Bank
older   oldest   younger   youngest

1-56822-908-9 *Building Grammar*

Name _____

Where Do You Live?

> The describing words *a, an,* and *the* are called **articles**.
>   *A* and *an* can mean any person or thing.
>   *I got **a** book.*
>   Use *an* in front of words that start with vowels: *a, e, i, o,* and *u.*
>   *An Eskimo lives in **an** igloo.*
>   **The** means a particular thing or things.
>   *I read **the** book that you read last week.*

Read each sentence and complete it by drawing a line to the correct description. Fill in the missing articles and finish each sentence.

1. I live where it is always cold, in a house that could melt.

   I am . . .

   ____ cage in ____ zoo.

2. I pace back and forth, back and forth. Sometimes I pace so fast you can't see my stripes through the bars on . . .

   ____ Eskimo in ____ igloo.

3. I live in New York City. My house is so tall it reaches to the clouds. I live in a building with lots of other people . . .

   ____ reservation.
   ____ Navajo.

4. My home is where it gets very hot. Sometimes my only neighbors are lizards.

   I live on . . .
   I am . . .

   in ____ apartment on ____ thirtieth floor.

Name _____

Describing Words

Adverbs are words that tell more about verbs. They tell **when**, **where**, or **how** an action takes place.

We eat indoors.
Indoors tells more about **where** we eat.

The race started late.
Late tells **when** the race started.

Runners work hard.
Hard tells **how** runners work.

Underline each adverb you find in the sentences below.

1. Grandma snores loudly.

2. Jamie leaves tomorrow.

3. Amy always sits here.

4. The baby eats often.

5. Animals are nearby.

6. My pony ran quickly.

7. Rafael drove slowly.

8. I will go to school later.

1-56822-908-9 *Building Grammar*

Name _____

To the Fair

> **Adverbs** tell more about verbs. They can tell **when**, **where**, or **how** an action takes place.
>
> Robbie rode *today*. (when)
> Robbie rode *outdoors*. (where)
> Robbie rode *slowly*. (how)

Read the following story. Underline each adverb that you find. **Hint:** there are 14 adverbs.

Grandma took me to the fair yesterday. We drove slowly in her car. Grandma honked her horn loudly. We drove far away.

The pigs at the fair squealed often. The cows mooed sadly. Horses pranced nearby. They danced gracefully.

I laughed cheerfully with the clowns. Nearby, Grandma won first place in the apple pie competition. She happily accepted the blue ribbon.

On the drive home, I fell asleep quickly. Grandma laid my head gently in her lap. When we got home, she tenderly put me to bed. We had an exciting day!

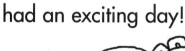

Try This Write a story about a trip you took. Make sure to use lots of adverbs.

Name _____

How in the World?

> **Adverbs** tell more about verbs. They can tell **when**, **where**, or **how** an action takes place.
>
> *I walked **today**. (when)*
> *I walked **nearby**. (where)*
> *I walked **quickly**. (how)*

Write **when**, **where**, or **how** on the line to show what each adverb tells.

1. I run **sometimes**. _____

2. Meredith walks **swiftly**. _____

3. My dog drinks **outside**. _____

4. Dan bikes **weekly**. _____

5. The car drove **slowly**. _____

6. My purse is **there**. _____

7. Joel plays **happily**. _____

8. Kate dives **next**. _____

9. Jacob reads **inside**. _____

10. I leap **gracefully**. _____

1-56822-908-9 *Building Grammar*

Name _____

When, Where, and How?

> **Adverbs** tell more about verbs. They help tell **when**, **where**, or **how** an action takes place.
>
> *I eat **often**. (when)*
> *I eat **nearby**. (where)*
> *I eat **quickly**. (how)*

Finish these sentences with adverbs. Your adverb must answer the question word in parentheses.

1. I skipped _____ down the lane. **(how)**

2. John walked his dog _____ . **(where)**

3. I will _____ brush my teeth. **(when)**

4. My family eats dinner _____ . **(how)**

5. Lucy dances _____ . **(how)**

6. We go to the movies _____ . **(when)**

7. Karen goes jogging _____ . **(when)**

8. I will walk _____ . **(where)**

Name _____

Monopoly Mania

A **pronoun** takes the place of a noun. Subject pronouns take the place of the subject in a sentence.

Roberto likes to play Monopoly.
He likes to play Monopoly.

Replace each bold noun with the correct subject pronoun. Choose from these subject pronouns: **I, you, he, she, it, we, they**. Write it on the line.

1. **Roberto** opens the Monopoly board. _____

2. **Julia** chooses the racing car as her playing piece. _____

3. Maria wants to be the banker. **Maria** likes math. _____

4. **Roberto and Michael** decide to take care of the real estate. _____

5. **Maria, Michael, Julia, and Roberto** roll the dice to see who goes first. _____

6. **Julia** rolls the highest number and starts the game. _____

7. **Roberto** rolls seven and goes to jail. _____

8. **Roberto** rolls three times before he rolls doubles and gets out of jail. _____

9. "Let's count our money to see who won," **Michael** says. _____

10. "Maria wins," **Roberto** says. "She has the most money." _____

Name _____

Lunch at the Creature Café

Pronouns take the place of nouns.

Katie and I = **we**
Katie, Jenny, and Sean = **they**
lasagna = **it**

Katie and Jenny made a date to meet at the Creature Café for lunch. Underline all the subject pronouns in Jenny's journal entry about their meal. Pronouns: **I, you, he, she, it, we, they**.

Saturday, January 27

Katie and I met at the Creature Café. We looked at the menu. It had funny creature names for the food. We were served Sizzling Snake Soup. There were no snakes. It was really made with noodles. We ate Leapin' Lizard Lasagna. It was yummy. For dessert, we had Penguin Popsicles. After we ate lunch, we hugged. We said we would meet for lunch next month. I waved goodbye as my friend Katie drove away.

Try This Write a journal entry of what happened today at lunch.

63

Name _____

It Is Missing

> A **pronoun** takes the place of a noun (person, place, or thing).
>   **person** = I, you, he, she, we, they
>   **thing or place** = it
>
>   *Mary* hid under the *table*.
>   *She* hid under *it*.

Write the correct pronoun on the line after each word in bold type to take the place of each noun.

King Riggle and His Missing Crown

Once upon a time in the land of Woggles, there was a king named Riggle. **King Riggle** _____ loved to wear his crown. **King Riggle** _____ even wore **the crown** _____ to bed. The only time he took the crown off was when he ate **his lunch** _____ . That was because **the crown** _____ always fell into his mashed potatoes.

One day the king's crown was missing.

"**The Woggles** _____ must find my crown!" King Riggle said.

All of the Woggles looked up and looked down the land. But **the Woggles** _____ did not find the king's crown. The gardener didn't find **the crown** _____ . **The butler** _____ who carried King Riggle's food to the table didn't find **the crown** _____ . However, the crown was found in the kitchen. Can you guess who found **the crown** _____ and where?

1-56822-908-9 *Building Grammar*

Name _____

For You

> **Object pronouns** replace the object of the sentence. They are usually in the last part of the sentence. They are: **me**, **you**, **her**, **him**, **them**, **us**, and **it**.
>
> *Molly gave the game to **us**.*
> *I wrote a note to **her**.*

Replace each object in the sentences below with an object pronoun. Write the pronoun on the line after each sentence. Remember, the object pronouns are: **me**, **you**, **her**, **him**, **them**, **us**, and **it**.

1. Kevin gave **Robert** a candy bar.   _____

2. I rode on **the bus**.   _____

3. Laurie tossed the ball to **Becky**.   _____

4. Sharon ate **the apple**.   _____

5. Roberto cheered for **Sue and Dan**.   _____

6. Janelle drove **David and me** to the fair.   _____

7. I walked **Mario** to school.   _____

8. Mrs. Walker gave **my class** a treat.   _____

65

Name _____

We're Together

Some words like **is** and **are** can be put together with other words to make **contractions**. The **i** of *is* or the **a** of *are* is dropped and added to a pronoun. They are connected by an apostrophe (').

     it + is = it's   *you + are = you're*

Remember: in a contraction, the whole first word is still there.

Draw a line from each pair of words to the correct contraction.

he is	I'm
they are	you're
we are	they're
she is	he's
I am	it's
you are	we're
it is	she's

   1-56822-908-9 *Building Grammar*

Name _____

We'll Work Together

A pronoun and the word **will** can be put together to make a shorter word called a **contraction**. An apostrophe (') takes the place of any letters left out.

Singular
I will = I'll
you will = you'll
he will = he'll

Plural
we will = we'll
they will = they'll

I will help Mary study.
I'll help Mary study.

Make the following letter shorter by writing a contraction on the line after each set of words in bold type.

Dear Mr. Woods,

Our class will help in the library. Here is the list of what **we will** _____ do:

Michelle will _____ organize the work crew schedule.

Sara and Henry will _____ pick up any trash.

We will _____ borrow your big broom to sweep the sidewalks.

Mario volunteered. **He will** _____ get big garbage bags.

Ronnie, Jay, and Katy will _____ help keep birds away from the construction area.

I will _____ let the work crews leave class 15 minutes early for recess.

You will _____ be happy with our work.

Sincerely,
Mrs. Alton

1-56822-908-9 *Building Grammar*

Name _____

Do not, Did not

A verb and the word **not** can be put together to make a shorter word called a **contraction**. An apostrophe (') takes the place of any letters left out.

is not = isn't   do not = don't
did not = didn't   are not = aren't

Write the contractions that can replace some of the words in Mary's letter to her friend. Write them above the old words.

Dear Jimmy,

Disneyland is not far from the beach. We did not ride a train to Disneyland. We drove our car. Disneyland did not open until 9 o'clock.

We did not agree on what to do first. Finally, we began our visit in Fantasyland. We did not want to miss any fun. We stayed until midnight. It was so much fun! I am sorry you could not go with us. If we take this trip again, my mother promised that you are not staying at home. You will come with us! Is not that exciting?

Your friend,

Mary

Name _____

Where's My Stuff?

> A verb and the word **not** can be put together to make a
> shorter word called a **contraction**. An apostrophe (') takes
> the place of any letters left out.
>
> *did not = didn't*

Greg had so many things in his backpack that it broke and everything spilled out. His friends were walking behind him. What did each friend find? Write the two words on the lines that make up each contraction. Then write what Greg's friend's found on the answer line.

1. "Who found my package with something I chew at recess?" asked Greg.

    "I didn't (_____ _____) find your gum, but I found something you write with on paper," said Jamie.

    Answer: _____

2. "I don't (_____ _____) have my compass. Who has it?" asked Greg.

    "I can't (_____ _____) find north or south, but I can get rid of wrong answers," said Emily.

    Answer: _____

3. "My yo-yo isn't (_____ _____) in my backpack," said Greg.

    "I don't (_____ _____) have it," said Jerry, "but I have something else to use at recess. There are at least 50 round balls. Some are clear. Some look like cats' eyes. Others are solid colors and stripes."

    Answer: _____

69

Name _____

Morning Message

> A **sentence** is a group of words that tells a complete idea about someone or something.
>
> *The girls are coming home. (sentence)*
> *The girls home (not a sentence)*

Mrs. Alton wrote a morning message to her class on the chalkboard. Some of her sentences don't make sense. Underline the sentences that don't tell a complete idea.

Today is Tuesday. It is the day after. This morning I will read a book. Its title is. The P.E. teacher will teach us to play soccer. Soccer is.

We will make a graph. Before we go home. You can check out three books.

Try This Can you fix the morning message for Mrs. Alton by putting in words to make her sentences complete?

1-56822-908-9 *Building Grammar*

Name _____

The Creature Café

A **sentence** is a group of words that tells a complete thought or idea.

John and Melanie eat red and green apples.(sentence)
eat red and green apples (not a sentence)

Find and underline the complete sentences in The Creature Café's Menu.

The Creature Café

Penguin Pizza
The pizza is made with
white cheese and black olives.
No Spaghetti Sauce

Cheetah Cheese Sandwich

Melted yellow cheese on
toasted white bread.

After you eat this sandwich,
you'll run like a cheetah.

Salads
Goat Cheese
Plain lettuce and tomato
are sprinkled with goat cheese.

Coyote Caesar
You'll howl when you taste this
special dressing.

Soups
Owl Onion
An owl would rather gulp it
up than snooze.

Pig n' Potato
Little chunks of ham and potato.
Warm and creamy.

Drinks
Raccoon's Raspberry Tea
Even with a mask, you can
taste the sweet raspberries
in this tea.

Lion Lemonade
This golden yellow juice
roars with sweetness.

Name _____

All Mixed Up

The **order** of the words in a sentence tells what the sentence means.

Sam the banana eats. (wrong)
The banana eats Sam. (wrong)
Sam eats the banana. (correct)

Draw a line from the picture to the sentence that makes sense.

1. The bag fell out of Sam's sandwich.
   Sam's sandwich fell out of the bag.

2. The dog ran after the ball.
   The ball ran after the dog.

3. Sam's candy bar melted the sun.
   The sun melted Sam's candy bar.

Try This Draw a silly picture of a mixed-up sentence.

1-56822-908-9 *Building Grammar*

Name _____

More Mix-Ups

> The **order** of the words in a sentence tells what the sentence means.
>
> *The cow milks the man.*   (wrong)
> *The man milks the cow.*   (right)

Draw a line from the picture to the sentence that makes sense.

1. Mary ate the cookies.
   The cookies ate Mary.

2. My skin burned the sun.
   The sun burned my skin.

3. The bunny ate the carrots.
   The carrots ate the bunny.

1-56822-908-9 *Building Grammar*

Name _____

Bulletin Board Mix-Up

> A sentence always starts with a **capital letter**.
> _The_ zebra lost its stripes.
> _He_ found them in the leopard's cage.

Circle the words on the "Star of the Week" board that need capital letters.

Star of the Week

Maria is tall.
she has black hair.

our star has a dog.
his name is Cleo.

disneyworld is her favorite place.
She likes Toon Town.

she likes to read books.

Try This Make a "Star of the Week" board for yourself. How many are in your family? What's your favorite food? Make sure all your sentences start with a capital letter and end with a period.

1-56822-908-9 _Building Grammar_

Name _____

My First Day

> Telling sentences end with a **period**. Periods are like stop signs. They tell you when a sentence ends.
>
> *The sentence ends here.*

Fix these sentences. Some need a period. Some need more words and a period. The missing words are in the Word Bank.

Word Bank

pizza	Mrs. Hill	class
friends	soccer	bus

1. I like school

2. My teacher's name is _____

3. I have three _____

4. At recess, we play _____

5. On Monday, we have music _____

6. My favorite food for lunch is _____

7. We are learning addition in math class

8. I ride the _____ to school

Try This Write your own story about school. Then give it to a friend to read. Did you remember all the periods?

1-56822-908-9 *Building Grammar*

Name _____

Snack Time

> A **telling sentence** tells something. It ends with a perod.
> *Ice cream is cold.*

Read each label and underline the telling sentences for each snack.

Puffy Potato Chips

These chips crunch when you eat them.

Made in the USA

Pineapple Chunks

The fruit is yellow and packed in water.

Banana Strawberry Swirl

This yogurt tastes better than ice cream.

String Cheese
Mozzarella

Each stick contains calcium and vitamins

Juiced-Up Juice

100% Natural Fruit

Juiced-up juice tastes like real fruit.

8 servings.

Uncle Doorbell's Popcorn

With butter and salt.

It tastes like movie popcorn.

1-56822-908-9 *Building Grammar*

Name _____

Rollin' at Recess

A **telling sentence** tells about someone or something. A telling sentence starts with a capital and ends with a period.

Molly is playing jacks.

Finish these telling sentences about some kids at recess. All the words you will need are in the Word Bank. The picture clues will help you.

The girl is

The boys are playing

The girls are jumping

Sara and Joel are

Word Bank

ball   swinging   reading   rope

1-56822-908-9 _Building Grammar_

Name _____

Marble Mania

An **asking sentence** asks a question. It always begins with a capital letter and ends with a question mark.

<u>W</u>hat did you bring for lunch today<u>?</u>

Write asking sentences to go with the picture below. Use the Word Bank for help.

Who _____?

What _____?

When _____?

Where _____?

Why _____?

Word Bank
marbles   recess   shady tree   lunches   circle

78

1-56822-908-9 *Building Grammar*

Name _____

Whom Do I Ask?

An **asking sentence** asks a question about something or someone. It always ends with a question mark.
Who will help me carry this heavy box?

Underline each asking sentence. Write answers from the Word Bank in the blanks.

1. I need a book to read. Who can help me find one?
   The _____ can help you find a book.

2. I cut my knee. Who can help me?
   The _____ can help you.

3. Who can teach me how to read?
   Your _____ will help you learn to read.

4. Who can help me clean up this milk?
   The _____ will bring his mop.

5. Who can teach me to play the violin?
   The _____ knows how to play.

6. Who can show me how to draw a picture of a zebra?
   The _____ can show you how to draw a zebra.

Word Bank
nurse   librarian   teacher   janitor
music teacher   art teacher

1-56822-908-9 *Building Grammar*

Name _____

I Have a Secret

> **Telling sentences** tell something. They end with a period(.).
>
> *I have a secret.*
>
> **Asking sentences** ask a question. They end with a question mark(?).
>
> *Do you want to know what it is?*

Put a period at the end of each telling sentence. Put a question mark at the end of each asking sentence.

1. I'll tell you

2. Do you promise not to tell anyone

3. Tomorrow is my birthday

4. Can you guess what I'm making for the class

5. I am baking cupcakes

6. Do you like chocolate or vanilla frosting

7. What kind of ice cream do you like

8. I think I know your answer

9. Should I ask Mrs. Alton if we can celebrate after math

80

Name _____

Hannah Hippo's Trip

An **asking sentence** asks a question. It ends with a **?**

Where is Hannah Hippo going?

A **telling sentence** tells something. It ends with a **.**

Hannah is going to Florida.

Decide if each sentence is asking or telling. Then put the correct punctuation at the end of each sentence.

Hannah Hippo
wants to go on
a trip

Should she ride
the bus or take
the train

Hannah Hippo
finally finds a
jumbo jet

Hannah lands in
Florida

Where is Auntie

Will Auntie get
there in time to
pick up Hannah

Try This   Finish the story of Hannah Hippo's trip with asking and telling sentences.

1-56822-908-9 *Building Grammar*

Name _____

Animal Jeopardy

> A **telling sentence** can be changed to an **asking sentence**.
>
> *Horses eat grass.*
> *What do horses eat?*

Change the telling sentences below to asking sentences. Remember the question mark (**?**) at the end of your asking sentence. The first one has been done for you.

1. A giraffe can eat leaves on tall trees.

   <u>What can a giraffe eat?</u>

2. Monkeys eat bananas.

   _____

3. Zebras look like horses with stripes.

   _____

4. Elephants are the biggest animals at the zoo.

   _____

5. Panda bears are from China.

   _____

6. Turtles live in shells.

   _____

1-56822-908-9 *Building Grammar*

Name _____

Sh-h-h-! Be Quiet.

Some sentences show strong feeling or surprise. They end with an exclamation point(!).

Its teeth are sharp<u>*!*</u>

Other sentences give a command or make a request. They end with a period(.).

Sit down in your seat<u>*.*</u>

If the sentence tells something exciting, put an exclamation mark (!) at the end. If it tells you to do something, put a period (.) at the end.

1. Oh no, the hungry lion is missing

2. Lock the gate so the others won't escape

3. His teeth are so sharp

4. Follow his tracks

5. Look, he's back

6. Find the key to his cage

7. Open the door

8. Put food in his cage

9. Wow, that was close

1-56822-908-9 *Building Grammar*

Name _____

Where in the World?

A sentence that gives a command or makes a request ends with a period. It usually tells **you** to do something.

Please shut the door.

Maria is telling her friend Emily how to get to her house. Finish the command sentences using the map to Maria's house.

Word Bank

school	Grass	Road	courts
Sky	park	Lake	Lucy

1. Walk to the _____ and get your bike.

2. Then turn right on _____ Lane.

3. Then turn right again on _____ Lane.

4. Ride past the _____ with the swings and slide.

5. Turn left when you see Smiley _____.

6. Ride along Lakeshore Drive, past _____ Sherwood.

7. Don't go past the tennis _____.

8. Turn right on _____ Avenue.

Tennis Courts

my house

Lucy Avenue

Lake Sherwood

Lakeshore Drive

Smiley Road

Sky Lane

park

Grass Lane

school

your bike

Name _____

.?!

> There are four kinds of sentences.
>   **Declarative (.)**—tells something
>   *I helped the librarian put away books.*
>   **Interrogative (?)**—asks a question
>   *Do you know how many books are in our library?*
>   **Exclamatory (!)**—makes a strong, surprised, or angry statement
>   *Wow, that box of books is heavy!*
>   **Imperative (.)**—gives a command or makes a request
>   *Help carry some of these boxes.*

Write the name of the kind of sentence on the line after each sentence. Then, put in the punctuation that belongs with each sentence.

1. Hooray, it's finally here _____

2. Our new library will open in two more days _____

3. Bring your parents to the dedication on Thursday _____

4. Do you know what time the dedication starts _____

5. It begins at ten o'clock _____

6. Tell them to be here early to get a good seat _____

7. Does the library look fantastic _____

8. We should all be proud _____

9. I'm so excited _____

Name _____

Pet Shop

Every sentence ends with a punctuation mark. **Statements**, **commands**, or **requests** end with a period. **Questions** end with a question mark. Sentences with strong feeling or emotion end with an exclamation mark.

I like to read.
Please pass the noodles.
Do you understand?
We won!

Put the correct punctuation mark at the end of each sentence.

1. Two dogs are in that cage ___

2. Oh no, a snake ___

3. My brother likes goldfish ___

4. Please don't feed the hamsters ___

5. Do you have a pet ___

6. Watch out ___

7. The parrots are loose ___

8. Do these fish cost a lot ___

9. May I have a cat ___

10. That cat is pretty ___

1-56822-908-9 *Building Grammar*

Name _____

Goodnight . ? !

> Sentences must have proper punctuation marks at the end.
> **Periods** end sentences that make statements.
> > *Someone is at my door_.*
> **Question marks** end sentences that ask questions.
> > *Who is at my door_?*
> **Exclamation marks** end sentences that show strong feeling or emotion.
> > *When I saw the bear, I fainted_!*

Maria's mother is trying to get the kids at the campout to go to sleep. Place the correct punctuation mark on the line at the end of each sentence.

11:00 P.M.   Maria's mother walks outside, smiling ___
    "Do you kids know what time it is ___
    It's time for lights out ___ "

11:15 P.M.   Maria's mother walks outside, frowning ___
    "Second warning ___
    You may still whisper ___
    Do you know how to whisper ___ "

11:30 P.M.   Maria's mother and father walk out together ___
    They are both frowning ___
    "This is your third warning ___
    No more whispering or giggling ___
    Close your eyes ___
    You have an early soccer game tomorrow ___
    Get to sleep ___ "

12:00 A.M.   Maria's father comes out alone ___
    He's rubbing his head ___
    "The next person I hear goes home ___
    Goodnight ___ "

1-56822-908-9 *Building Grammar*

Name _____

Together at Last

Two sentences can be joined together if their ideas
are alike. When you join sentences, add **and**, **or**, or **but**.
   Mary hugs her sister. + *Mary leaves.*
   Mary hugs her sister and leaves.

See if you can combine these pairs of sentences into one sentence. Write
the new sentence on the line.

1. Jerry has five balls. + Jerry has two bats.

_____

2. Sara baked cookies. + Sara baked muffins.

_____

3. The dog ran. + The dog barked.

_____

4. My mom loves books. + My mom loves pictures.

_____

     1-56822-908-9 *Building Grammar*

Name _____

Let's Get Together

> Join two sentences if their ideas are similar by using **and**, **or**, or **but**.
>
> *Betsy tickles the baby.* + *Betsy giggles.*
> *Betsy tickles the baby and giggles.*

Combine each pair of sentences into one sentence. Write the new sentence on the line.

1. Alyson jumped down. ➕ Alyson tripped.

_____

2. The squirrel grabbed the nut. ➕ The squirrel ran.

_____

3. My dad mows the lawn. ➕ My dad clips the hedges.

_____

4. I love to read books. ➕ I love to read magazines.

_____

Name _____

The I's Have It

> When you talk about yourself, you use the word **I**. You are important, so **I** is always capitalized. Remember, when **I** stands alone, it is always capitalized.
>
> *I had fun at recess.*
> *Jack and I played on the swings.*

It's recess. Your friend wrote you a secret note. To find out what he said, fill in the blanks with either a capital *I* or a small *i*.

___ have a surpr___se for us after school. Could you come to my house? ___t will be fun! You and ___ could make cook___es. ___ like to bake. Do you?

___ will call my mother at recess. She w___ll pick us up after school. ___ think she might take us to get ___ce-cream cones too. ___ like Cook___es and Cream. What ___ce-cream flavor do you l___ke best?

Later, ___ think we will play ball. ___ have a box full of bats, balls, and gloves.

Please say yes. ___ want you to be my friend.

Name _____

Logo Land

Special names of people and places are called **proper nouns**. They always begin with a capital letter.

Mr. Jones   *Disneyland*

Help Mr. Dibble, the city sign painter, fix the signs. Underline each word that needs a capital letter.

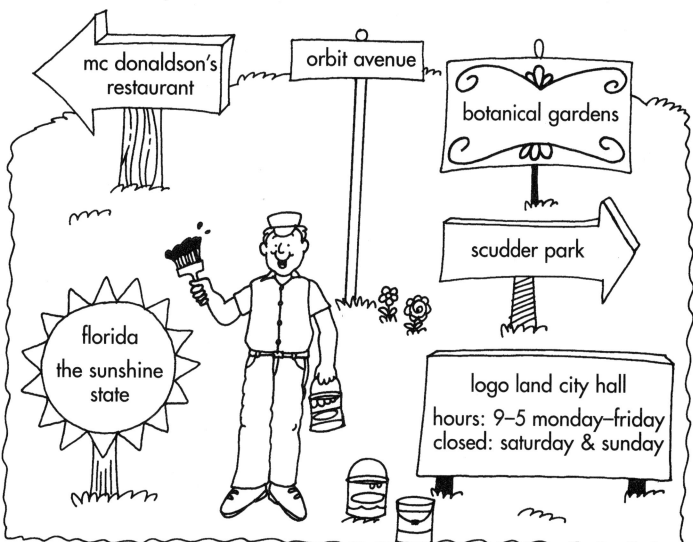

Try This   Make your own sign for your school or town.

Name _____

What's Missing?

> Names of specific people and places always begin with a capital letter. These are called **proper nouns**.
>
> **Patty** is my best friend. (name of a person)
> She lives in **California**. (name of a place)

This is a page from Kacie's phone book. She made some mistakes. She forgot the capitals for names and places. Can you help her fix them?

_____

jenny simon
69 black beauty drive
aspen, colorado 81611

_____

_____

_____

_____

aunt molly
562 compass circle
san diego, california 92101

_____

_____

_____

jeremy binner
8941 lakeshore drive
tempe, arizona 85280

_____

_____

Try This Start your own address book. Get the names, addresses, and phone numbers of family and friends and put them in alphabetical order. Don't forget the capital letters.

1-56822-908-9 *Building Grammar*

Name _____

A Name? A Name!

> The names of specific people and places begin with capital letters. These are called **proper nouns**.
>
> *George Washington*
> *Portland, Oregon*

Mrs. Poppins, the principal, has asked students at Pleasant Elementary School to suggest names for their new library. Circle each word below that needs a capital letter.

1. The library should be named the book market.—Lisa

2. Name it babe ruth library.—Jeremy

3. The library's new name should be the land of adventure.
   sara nagel

4. Let's name it the friendship library.—jenny wagner

5. We could use the big apple, new york city's nickname, for our library.
   Sean Carpenter

6. Libraries are places to be quiet and read. Let's name it quiet zone.
   Mike from mrs. alton's class

7. The pleasant elementary school library should be named after someone who writes books, such as louisa may alcott, beverly cleary, tomie de paola, or shel silverstein.—Teresa

Name _____

Calendar Capers

Proper nouns include days of the week, months of the year, and special holidays. They always begin with a capital letter.

Thanksgiving is always on the last Thursday in November.

Using the Word Bank below, write the month at the top of the calendar. Fill in the missing days of the week. Ask your teacher to help you number the calendar for the current year. Write in the special holidays for the month.

		Tuesday			Friday	

Word Bank

saturday	monday	thursday	sunday	wednesday
december	christmas	hanukkah	new year's eve	
kwanza				

1-56822-908-9 _Building Grammar_

Name _____

First, Last, and Important

Titles of books, movies, and TV shows are always capitalized. Capitalize the first, last, and important words in the title.

The Cat in the Hat
Alexander and the Terrible, Horrible, No Good, Very Bad Day

Circle the words in the titles that need capital letters.

1. the wizard of oz

2. beauty and the beast

3. the mouse detectives

4. jack and the beanstalk

5. the very hungry caterpillar

6. curious george

7. aladdin

8. pancakes for breakfast

1-56822-908-9 *Building Grammar*

Name _____

I'm From . . .

> Just like your name, the names of cities and states are **proper nouns** and must have capital letters. A comma goes between the city name and the state name.
>
> *Detroit, Michigan*

First, write the name of your city and state below. Don't forget the capital letters and the comma.

_____

Next, write the names of the following cities and states with capital letters and commas.

1. phoenix arizona _____

2. fargo north dakota _____

3. boise idaho _____

4. buffalo new york _____

5. macon georgia _____

6. st. louis missouri _____

7. san antonio texas _____

8. eureka california _____

Name _____

Teeny, Weeny Calendar

Sometimes we **abbreviate** the names of the days of the week or the names of the months of the year. May, June, and July are very short and do not need to be abbreviated. Every abbreviation ends with a period.

Mon. = Monday   *Jan. = January*

Fit the days of the week on this teeny, weeny calendar. Pick your favorite month of the year; their abbreviations are listed for you in the Word Bank below.

Word Bank

Jan.	Mar.	May	June
Apr.	Sept.	Feb.	Dec.
Nov.	Oct.	July	Aug.

Try This   Design your own teeny, weeny pocket calendar.

1-56822-908-9 *Building Grammar*

Name _____

A Postcard Reminder

Commas set apart the names of a city and state.

I live in New York City, New York. (in sentences)

25 W. Fifth Ave.
New York City, New York (in addresses on letters)

A list with more than two people, places, or things also needs commas between each item in the list.

Please bring a pair of tennis shoes, a sleeping bag, a water bottle, and a snack.

The kids going to the campout got a postcard telling them what to bring. Put commas where they belong in the message and the address.

Molly,
   You need to bring a sleeping bag a toothbrush a pillow and a bag of chips.

                    Becky

Molly Sleepy
52 Brown St.
Seattle WA 98101

Annie,
   You're in charge of games. Bring backgammon chess checkers and your fortune-telling cards.
                    Becky

Annie Awake
19 Green Grove Dr.
Seattle WA 98101

1-56822-908-9 *Building Grammar*

Name _____

Get in Line!

> When you have a list of three or more you must put **commas** between each item in the list.
>
> *I bought apples, oranges, peaches, and grapes.*

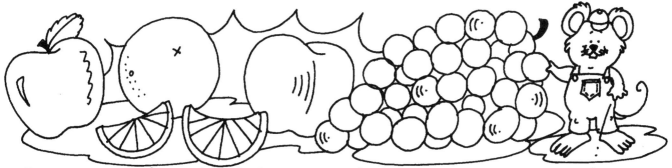

Put commas where they belong in each sentence below.

1. Katie Dan and Bobby played together.

2. It rained on Wednesday Thursday and Friday.

3. I have been to Michigan Ohio Iowa and New York.

4. Today we will study math science reading and music.

5. I like to ski skate and sled in the winter.

6. My favorite foods are carrots apples cookies and chips.

7. Sara needs her pencil paper crayons and scissors.

8. Today we will read draw and listen to stories.

Name _____

Star Gazers

> **Quotation marks** are used to show what people say.
> *"I saw two shooting stars!" yelled Robert.*

Put quotation marks where they belong in the sentences below.

1. Let's go star gazing,   Mom said.

2. I want the telescope!   Janelle yelled.

3. Keisha screamed,   No you don't!

4. Do you see any stars?   Janelle asked from behind Keisha.

5. I see Venus,   Mom exclaimed.

6. Where is it?   asked Dad.

7. There. Mom pointed up.   It's just behind that great big tree.

8. I see it,   Janelle proclaimed, shoving Keisha out of the way.

9. Oh no you don't.   Janelle pushed back.

10. Not again,   sighed Dad.

11. Girls will be girls,   Mom replied.

Name _____

Are You Talking to Me?

Quotation marks are used to set off the exact words of a speaker.

"Listen Mark," said John. "Did you hear that?"

Put quotation marks around what Mrs. Poppins said and what the students said.

1. I am here to get some ideas for our new library, Mrs. Poppins said.

2. I'd like a skylight, said Jenny.

3. H-m-m, said Mrs. Poppins. In her notebook she wrote what Jenny said.

4. I think we need a corner with lots of big, fluffy pillows, Tim said.

5. H-m-m, said Mrs. Poppins, and she wrote down what Tim said.

6. Lots and lots of books! yelled Maria.

7. H-m-m, said Mrs. Poppins. She wrote in her book what Maria said.

8. I'd like a computer to check out books, said a voice in the back.

9. Mrs. Poppins looked up. She saw the librarian, Miss Page. I think we can do that, Mrs. Poppins replied.

 1-56822-908-9 *Building Grammar*

Name _____

Hello, Goodbye!

> A letter starts with **greeting** words (Dear) and ends with **closing** words (Love).
>
> *Dear Nancy,*
> *How was your trip?*
> *Love,*
> *John*

Write greetings, closings, and names on the line for each letter. Some suggestions are at the bottom of the page.

_____ _____,

I miss you! I wish you would move back. Second grade isn't the same without you.

_____ ,

_____

_____ _____,

Please come to my birthday party on Saturday.

_____ ,

_____

_____ _____,

I tried your cereal. It was great. I got some at the store. Do you like yogurt?

_____ ,

_____

_____ _____,

How are you? Will you be coming for the summer? Mom is so excited. Call us and tell us when your plane arrives.

_____ ,

_____

Greetings	Closings
Dear _____,	Love,
Hi _____,	Missing you,
Dear Sir,	Sincerely,
Hey friend,	

1-56822-908-9 *Building Grammar*

Name _____

Dear . . .

When you write a letter, you must include certain things. You must have: a **date**, a **greeting**, a **body**, a **closing**, and a **signature**.

April 21 ◄—— **date**

greeting ——► *Dear Jane,*

I miss you! ◄—— **body**

closing ——► *Love,*

Bob ◄—— **signature**

On the form below, write a letter to a friend or family member. Remember to include all the elements of a letter.

_____

_____

_____

_____

_____

_____

_____

_____

_____

_____

_____

Answer Key

Who's First in Line?

Write the correct name on each line. The first letter has been written for you. When you are done, the names will be in **alphabetical order**. Three names are done already.

Angela	Bobby	Carrie	Dustin
Edward	Faith	Gloria	Holly
Ian	Jessica	Karen	Larry
Manuel	Nancy	Oliver	Patty
Quincy	Richie	Shelley	Tony
Ursula	Victor	Wendy	Xavier
Yolanda	Zoe		

Jessica	Larry	Karen	Faith	Gloria
Zoe	Holly	~~Dustin~~	Ursula	Patty
Carrie	Manuel	Nancy	Bobby	~~Shelly~~
Wendy	Ian	Xavier	Oliver	~~Quincy~~
Tony	Richie	Angela	Edward	Victor
Yolanda				

Page 4

Which Comes First?

Circle the first letter of each word. Then, write the words in each box in alphabetical order.

(A)pple (C)hair	(M)ap (L)eaf	(G)irl (B)ook
1. apple 2. chair	1. leaf 2. map	1. book 2. girl

(S)un (R)ing	(H)and (C)loud	(D)og (R)adio
1. ring 2. sun	1. cloud 2. hand	1. dog 2. radio

Page 5

Putting the Books Back

When the first letter of two words is the same, you need to use the second letter of the words to decide which word comes first.

Which book comes first?
Black Beauty or *Brown Bear*

Think: 1. Both names start with B.
2. The second letter in *Black Beauty* is l.
3. The second letter in *Brown Bear* is r.
4. l comes before r in alphabetical order, so *Black Beauty* comes before *Brown Bear*.

Use the numbers 1–12 to show the alphabetical order of these books. You may need to use scratch paper to figure it out.

8	One Fine Day	6	Nate the Great
11	Snakes are Nothing to Sneeze At	12	Sylvester and the Magic Pebble
1	Charlotte's Web	5	Fox in Socks
4	Don't Touch	7	No Such Things
10	Pickle Juice	3	Dinosaur Time
2	Cloudy with a Chance of Meatballs	9	Owls in the Family

Try This Alphabetize your classroom library or your books at home.

Page 6

Nouns Name Things

A **noun** is a word that names a thing.
paper, crayon

Write the correct noun for each object under its picture. You may use the Word Bank for help.

1. pillow

4. glass

2. desk

5. chair

3. book

6. pencil

Word Bank		
desk	pillow	chair
glass	book	pencil

Page 7

Published by Instructional fair. Copyright protected.

1-56822-908-9 *Building Grammar*

Writing the Naming Part

> **Nouns** name people, places, and things.
> *the boy = person*
> *the supermarket = place*
> *a tent = thing*

Write one of the nouns from the fort on each line to begin each sentence.

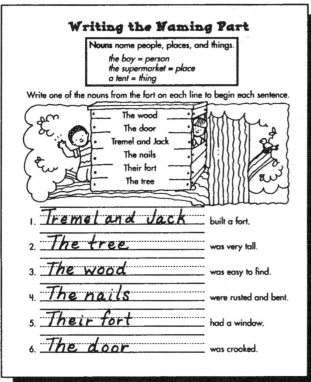

The wood
The door
Tremel and Jack
The nails
Their fort
The tree

1. *Tremel and Jack* ____ built a fort.
2. *The tree* ____ was very tall.
3. *The wood* ____ was easy to find.
4. *The nails* ____ were rusted and bent.
5. *Their fort* ____ had a window.
6. *The door* ____ was crooked.

Page 8

Munchin' on Lunch

> **Nouns** name people, places, and things.
> *boy, teacher = people*
> *playground, classroom = places*
> *jump rope, lunch bag = things*

Circle all the nouns below. Draw a line from each noun that could go in your lunch to the bag.

napkin
apple
hot
carrots
red
cracker

milk
hill
cookie
clouds
cheese
Dad

Page 9

Aimee's Day

> **Nouns** can name people, places, and things.
> *Aimee = person*
> *school = place*
> *chips = thing*

Circle all the nouns in the sentences below.

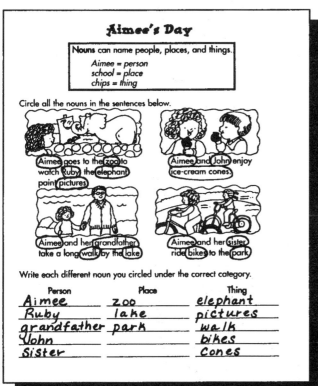

Aimee goes to the zoo to watch Ruby the elephant paint pictures.

Aimee and John enjoy ice-cream cones.

Aimee and her grandfather take a long walk by the lake.

Aimee and her sister ride bikes to the park.

Write each different noun you circled under the correct category.

Person	Place	Thing
Aimee	zoo	elephant
Ruby	lake	pictures
grandfather	park	walk
John		bikes
sister		cones

Page 10

Let's Go on a Nature Hike!

> **Nouns** name people, places, or things.
> *Rachel = person*
> *trail = place*
> *rock = thing*

Find the nouns in the wordsearch that might be seen on a nature hike. Oops! There are some words in the bank that aren't nouns. Cross those out first.

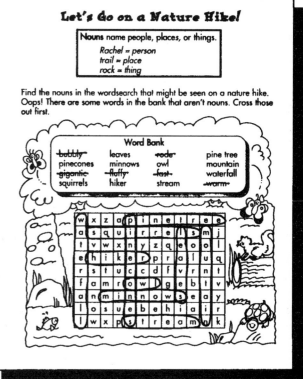

Word Bank

bubbly   leaves   rude   pine tree
pinecones   minnows   owl   mountain
gigantic   fluffy   fast   waterfall
squirrels   hiker   stream   warm

Page 11

105

1-56822-908-9 *Building Grammar*

One Pencil, Two Erasers

Many nouns for people, places, and things add **s** to the end to show more than one. These are called **plural nouns**.

I have one pencil, two erasers, and ten crayons.

Pete and Sara are cleaning their desks. Help them make a list of the school tools they have. Remember to add an **s** when there is more than one. Write the number and the name of the tool on the lines.

 2 erasers

 6 crayons

 4 pencils

 1 ruler

3 bottles of glue

 5 books

Page 12

Knock! Knock!

To make a word that names more than one person, place, or thing, you sometimes add **s** to the end. This is called a **plural noun**.

boy	*girl*
plural = boys	plural = girls

Write down who has come to your door. Remember to add an **s** when there is more than one. Use the Word Bank for help. The first one has been done for you.

Knock! Knock!

Who's There?

1. Two boys on <u>bicycles</u> are here.

2. Mary brought a cage with six **birds**.

3. Two **dogs** are riding their skateboards.

4. A lady has nine **balloons** for the party.

5. Uh! Oh! These **clowns** came to the wrong party.

Word Bank

balloon   clown   dog
bird   ~~bicycle~~

Page 13

Jobs Galore

A plural noun names more than one person, place, or thing. When a noun ends in a consonant followed by the letter **y**, change the final **y** to **i** and add **es**.

story = stories   sky = skies   penny = pennies

The kids at Pleasant School thought of some ideas to raise money. Write the plural form of the correct noun on each line. The Word Bank will help you.

1. Ben and Maria had three pizza **parties**

2. On Saturday, Mrs. Alton's class took care of **babies**.

3. The students brought in their extra **pennies**.

4. The fifth-grade students read **stories** for fifty cents each.

5. School **families** donated money from yard sales.

6. Other **libraries** gave extra books.

Word Bank

party   baby   library
story   family   penny

Page 14

Where Are My Things?

To make some nouns plural, we add **es**. We add **es** to nouns that end with these letters:

s as in grass (grasses)	**sh** as in dish (dishes)
x as in box (boxes)	**ch** as in lunch (lunches)

To find out where forgetful Frank put his school supplies, write the plural ending (**s** or **es**) of each word on the line. Then find the words in the wordsearch.

He put his glass **es** in one of his pocket **s**

He left his pencil **s** and two of his book **s** at the reading table. He put the book about fox **es** on the box **es** in the library. When the bell rang, he carried the box with all the lunch **es** for all the children in both second grade class **es** to the tree **s** on the playground.

Page 15

Published by Instructional fair. Copyright protected.

1-56822-908-9 *Building Grammar*

Page 16

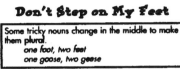

Don't Step on My Feet

Some tricky nouns change in the middle to make them plural.
one foot, two feet
one goose, two geese

See if you can find the tricky plural for each of the nouns below. Use the answers to fill in the crossword puzzle.

Across

2. A sign posted on the fence said: No _children_ (child) beyond this point.
3. Mr. Wood had 50 _men_ (man) working on the library building.
5. Is your foot on my _feet_ (foot)?
7. There are also four _women_ (woman) on the crew.

Down

1. About 30 _mice_ (mouse) scurried out.
4. Many _people_ (person) came to the dedication.
6. Did you lose your front _teeth_ (tooth)?

Page 17

That's Mine

Add 's to the end of a word to show that something belongs to someone. This is called a possessive noun.
Carol's cat is small.

Underline the possessive noun in each sentence. Draw a line to match each sentence with the correct picture.

1. Janie's hair is curly.
2. That wagon is Jacob's.
3. The bike's tire is flat.
4. The dog's ears are floppy.
5. That is the kitten's ball.

Try This — Write down the names of objects in your classroom. Now write sentences that tell to whom the objects belong. Make sure to use possessive nouns.

Page 18

Whose?

Add 's (apostrophe + s) to the end of a word to show that something belongs to someone. This is called a possessive noun.
That bike belongs to Sandy.
That is Sandy's bike.

Write the correct noun in each blank.

Marta's p.j.'s are red.
Marta   Martas   Marta's

This is _Joel's_ toothbrush.
Joels   Joel   Joel's

My _brother's_ ball is missing.
brother's   brothers   brother

That _girl's_ dress is pretty.
girl   girl's   girls

The _school's_ bell is broken.
schools   school's   school

This is the _dog's_ bone.
dog's   dog   dogs

The _class's_ teacher is Ms. Popp.
class   classes   class's

The _bear's_ fur is soft.
bear   bear's   bears

Page 19

Breakfast at the Creature Café

Nouns name people, places, or things.
A lizard with one eye is on the wall.
Verbs tell what someone or something is doing.
A lizard climbs the wall.

Read each sentence. Underline the nouns. Read each sentence again. Circle the verbs.

1. Lizards leap onto our table.
2. Monkeys swing down for bananas.
3. Giraffes stretch their necks and nibble some leaves.
4. Wart hogs slurp their oatmeal.
5. The goats lick our plates clean.
6. A chimp rings up our bill.

Try This — Write a story about a crazy breakfast.

1-56822-908-9 *Building Grammar*

Rockin' at Recess

> **Verbs** show action.
> *I run to school everyday.*
> *Josh hides in the bushes.*

Look for the following action words in the wordsearch below: jump, swing, climb, hide, run, catch, and leap. The picture clues around the wordsearch will help you find the words.

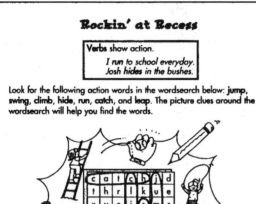

c	a	t	c	h	i	d
t	h	r	l	k	u	e
x	y	c	i	s	m	r
r	u	n	m	w	p	l
m	f	j	b	i	m	e
x	a	q	b	n	w	a
h	i	d	e	g	y	p

Try This Draw a picture. See how many verbs (action words) you can draw.

Animal Action

> **Verbs** tell us what is happening in a sentence. Some verbs show lots of action:
> *walk, run, jump, hop, eat, swing, pick, fly, climb*
> Other verbs tell about things we do:
> *look, talk, read, hear, think, live*

Write in the missing verb in each sentence below. You can find all the verbs you will need in the examples at the top of the page.

1. Can rabbits __*jump*__ higher than kangaroos?
2. Can elephants __*pick*__ up peanuts with their trunks?
3. Do monkeys __*swing*__ from tree to tree using their tails?
4. Can a lion __*climb*__ a tree?
5. How far can a hummingbird __*fly*__ each day?
6. Could a penguin __*live*__ in the desert?
7. When can you __*hear*__ a coyote howling?
8. What doctor could __*talk*__ to the animals?

Animals Move

> **Verbs** show the action in a sentence. Verbs tell what someone or something does.
> *Tamara ran out of school.*

Read each sentence and underline the verbs. Then find each verb in the wordsearch. Hint: There are twelve different verbs in the wordsearch.

Monkeys <u>swing</u> from tree to tree.
An alligator <u>swims</u> in the swamp.
Tarantulas <u>crawl</u> across rocks and sand.
Some snakes can <u>slither</u> up trees.
Other snakes <u>wriggle</u> in water.
Some kangaroos can <u>hop</u> more than 25 feet!

s	l	u	r	p	g	f	s
t	v	m	e	w	c	d	l
p	s	c	u	r	r	y	e
h	l	b	g	i	a	t	e
s	w	i	n	g	w	h	p
w	p	o	p	g	l	o	s
i	a	m	b	l	e	v	h
m	x	a	v	e	u	e	e
s	l	i	t	h	e	r	r

Armadillos <u>amble</u> slowly when eating ants.
Prairie dogs <u>pop</u> out of their holes and <u>scurry</u> around for food.
Grizzly bears <u>sleep</u> in their caves all winter.
Hummingbirds <u>hover</u> like helicopters and slurp nectar from flowers.

Saving the Planet

> Add **s** to a verb that tells what one person, animal, or thing does.
> *The boy helps the earth by recycling.*
> Do not add **s** to verbs to tell what two or more people, animals, or things do.
> *The boys help the earth by recycling.*

Copy the correct verb (a. or b.) for each sentence onto the writing lines.

1. Many kids _____ aluminum cans.
   a. collect b. collects
   collect

2. The girl _____ to recycle them.
   a. wants b. want
   wants

3. Boys and girls _____ newspapers.
   a. save b. saves
   save

4. Jack _____ old magazines to be recycled.
   a. bring b. brings
   brings

5. Some boys _____ old telephone books.
   a. gathers b. gather
   gather

1-56822-908-9 *Building Grammar*

1, 2, 3 Strikes You're Out!

A verb must agree in number with the subject of the sentence. If the subject of the sentence is one, add an s to the verb.

She plays with Ryan.

If the subject of the sentence is more than one, the verb does not need an s.

They play with Ryan.

Read each sentence out loud. Ask yourself if the sentence has one or more than one. Underline the correct verb and write it on the line.

1. The first batter **runs** (run, <u>runs</u>) to first base.

2. The next batter **swings** (<u>swings</u>, swing) at a low ball.

3. The right fielder **drops** (drop, <u>drops</u>) the ball.

4. The batter **scores** (score, <u>scores</u>) a run.

5. The pitcher **walks** (walk, <u>walks</u>) three Cubs.

6. The next two players **strike** (<u>strike</u>, strikes) out.

7. The last Cub **hits** (hit, <u>hits</u>) a home run.

8. The Cubs on all four bases **score** (<u>score</u>, scores).

Library Help

The ending of a verb tells whether it is in present or past tense. Present tense is what's happening now.

I pack books in boxes.

Past tense is what happened in the past.

I packed books in boxes yesterday.

Write the correct verb in each sentence.

1. Last week Mrs. Poppins **toured** (tours, toured) the library.

2. Yesterday, I **helped** (help, helped) Mrs. Alden stack books.

3. I love to **write** (write, wrote) stories.

4. The janitor **washed** (washes, washed) the floor yesterday.

5. José **put** (puts, put) books on the shelf today.

6. Amelia **cleaned** (cleans, cleaned) the tables just a few minutes ago.

7. The bulldozers **left** (leave, left) the school this morning.

8. I **sit** (sit, sat) in a bean-bag chair and watch.

Yesterday We Played

Some verbs add ed to the end to tell about action that happened in the past. These are called past tense verbs.

Today I play with Angela.
Yesterday I played with Sam.

Fill in this journal entry with verbs from the Word Bank below.

Word Bank

bicycled	rolled	laughed
fished	wanted	giggled
	looked	

Monday, August 14

Julie's Journal

Yesterday my family and I **bicycled** to the park. Mom made fried chicken, a green salad, and rolls. After eating, my Dad and I **fished** in the lake. My little sister **rolled** down the hill. She **laughed** and **giggled**. At three o'clock we **wanted** dessert. We got on our bikes and **looked** for an ice-cream shop. What do you think my favorite flavor is?

Guess What We Did

Many action words that tell what happened in the past tense end in ed.

Bob and Mary visit their friend.
Yesterday, Bob and Mary visited their friend.

Read what each group of kids did yesterday during lunch. Underline the past tense verbs that end in ed in each story. The group with the most verbs in the past tense (ed) did the safest thing.

Group 1

At recess we <u>played</u> on the playground. Mrs. Alton's cell phone <u>buzzed</u>. She <u>waved</u> her hands. Everyone <u>stopped</u> playing.

Mrs. Alton <u>yelled</u>, "Fire!"

We <u>noticed</u> the fire was in the garbage can. We <u>walked</u> to the hose and <u>turned</u> it on. Before the firemen <u>arrived</u>, we put out the fire. The bell rang. We went back to class.

Group 2

At lunch, we <u>started</u> walking to the cafeteria. Suddenly, Mrs. Alton <u>yelled</u>, "Fire!"

The fire truck sirens <u>screamed</u>. The men <u>shouted</u> to each other. They <u>unrolled</u> the hoses. They <u>turned</u> on the water. The firemen <u>sprayed</u> the garbage can. The fire was put out. We <u>walked</u> to the cafeteria. We <u>gobbled</u> our food and <u>walked</u> to recess.

Which group has the most action words in past tense (ed)?

Group #: **2**

I'm Gonna . . .

To talk about what is going to happen later, put a special verb, called a **helping verb**, in front of the regular verb. The helping verb used to talk about the future is **will**.

I walk home. (now)
I will walk home. (later)

Change the sentences below so they say what is going to happen later. The first one is done for you.

1. NOW: I eat apples.

   LATER: I will eat apples.

2. NOW: Mary rides her bike.

   LATER: Mary will ride her bike.

3. NOW: Josh loves chocolate.

   LATER: Josh will love chocolate.

4. NOW: The baby cries.

   LATER: The baby will cry.

5. NOW: I jump rope.

   LATER: I will jump rope.

The Zoo Album

Linking verbs link the first part of a sentence to the last part. They do not show action.

The wolf is in the largest cage.
Three wolves are in the largest cage.
I am afraid of wolves.

Underline the linking verb in each sentence.

1. The giant tortoise <u>is</u> green with brown and green spots.

2. The alligators <u>are</u> smaller than the giant tortoises.

3. The hippo and giraffe <u>are</u> next to each other.

4. This zebra <u>is</u> friendly.

5. I <u>am</u> the zookeeper at Park Zoo.

6. I <u>am</u> also the head tour guide.

7. Park Zoo <u>is</u> very large.

8. Harmony Farm is a great attraction at the zoo.

Jump, Hop, and Run

Linking verbs link the first part of a sentence to the last part. They do not show action.

The giraffe is the tallest animal at Park Zoo.
The turtles are the slowest animals at the zoo.

Read each sentence to yourself. Write the correct linking verb in each sentence. If the subject is singular (one), use **is**. If the subject is plural (more than one), use **are**.

1. The wolf _is_ in the cage next to the coyote.

2. The polar bears and the penguins _are_ in a new part of Park Zoo called Winter Express.

3. Owls and bats _are_ some of the nighttime animals at the zoo.

4. The zebra _is_ the animal that looks like a horse with stripes.

5. The monkeys _are_ the funniest animals at Park Zoo.

Stop! Halt! Whoa!

Synonyms are words that mean almost the same thing.

the scary tiger = the frightening tiger
the nice zookeeper = the pleasant zookeeper

Use the Word Bank to find new words that mean almost the same thing as the underlined words. Write them on the lines.

Lions have a loud <u>growl</u>. roar

You can see the monkeys <u>sway</u> from tree to tree. swing

Giraffes <u>select</u> leaves from tall trees. choose

Listen! Wolves <u>wail</u> at night. howl

Careful! A snake may <u>slide</u> into your lunch. slither

Word Bank
choose   slither   swing   howl   roar

110

Like Another

Synonyms are different words that mean almost the same thing.

Huge is another way to say big.

Fill in the crossword puzzle with words that mean the same as the underlined words in the sentences. Use the Word Bank for help.

Word Bank

friends
lead
last
shortest

gloomy
offer
marvelous
cheerful

Across

5. Matt is going to <u>guide</u> us to the gym.
6. Our teacher bakes <u>wonderful</u> treats.
8. That was the <u>final</u> question on the spelling test.

Down

1. I play tag with my <u>pals</u>.
2. I will <u>give</u> some of my chips to Cate.
3. I like books with <u>happy</u> endings.
4. It is very <u>dreary</u> outside today.
7. My sister is the <u>smallest</u> student in third grade.

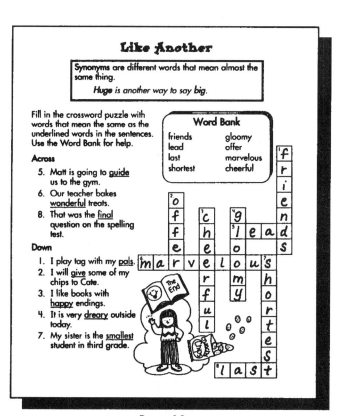

Page 32

Outside In, Inside Out

Antonyms are words that mean the opposite of each other.

Inside is the opposite of outside.

Circle each word that is the opposite of each picture.

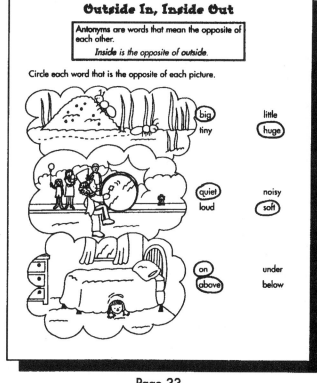

big   little
tiny   huge

quiet   noisy
loud   soft

on   under
above   below

Page 33

The Turtle n' the Hare

Antonyms are words that mean the opposite of each other.

Hot is the opposite of cold.

Look at each picture. Draw a line to the sentence that is the opposite.

Giraffes have <u>long</u> necks so they can eat leaves in <u>tall</u> trees.

Ellie the Elephant has <u>big</u> ears.

Polar bears have <u>white</u> fur to look like snow.

A jackrabbit's ears are very <u>thin</u> and <u>long</u>.

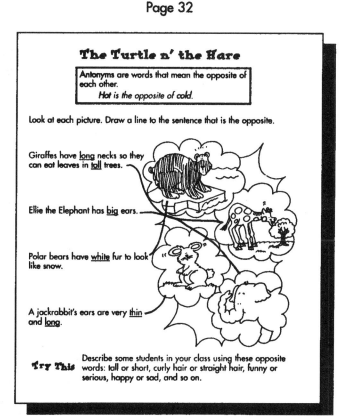

Try This Describe some students in your class using these opposite words: tall or short, curly hair or straight hair, funny or serious, happy or sad, and so on.

Page 34

I Rode on a Road

Homophones are words that sound alike but are spelled differently and have different meanings.

Ate means to eat yesterday.
Eight is a number that tells how many.

Match the pictures and words that sound the same by drawing a line.

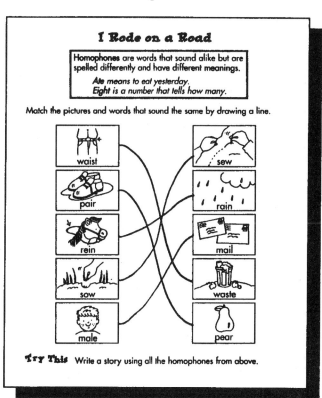

waist   sew
pair   rain
rein   mail
sow   waste
male   pear

Try This Write a story using all the homophones from above.

Page 35

What We Ate at Eight

> Homophones are words that sound alike but are spelled differently and have different meanings.
>
> **See means to look at something.**
> **Sea means the same as ocean.**

Find the correct word to use in each part of the sentence. Then write it on the line.

1. _Eight_ of us went to Burger-matic where we _ate_ hamburgers and French fries. (eight, ate)

2. The bus _fare_ for the ride to the county _fair_ was 50¢. (fair, fare)

3. Your _nose_ _knows_ what we will have for dinner. (knows, nose)

4. The doctor said my _heel_ will _heal_ faster if I keep it uncovered. (heel, heal)

5. Did you _write_ the invitation with your left or _right_ hand? (right, write)

6. _I_ notice you have one blue and one brown _eye_. (I, eye)

Try This Write a story using the homophones above.

Page 36

To, Two, Too, or TuTu

> To, two, and too are words we use a lot. Each one has a different meaning.
>
> **To** is a word used in front of a verb.
> *I like to camp.*
>
> **Two** is a number word.
> *I have two candy bars in my sleeping bag.*
>
> **Too** means *more than enough*, and is also used to mean *also*.
> *I had too much chocolate.* (more than enough)
> *My friend is going to the campout, too.* (also)

Write the correct to, two, or too in the blanks to finish these sentences.

1. Before you go _to_ sleep, brush your teeth.

2. I'm hungry. I want _two_ more candy bars.

3. Uh! Oh! I'm _too_ big for this chair.

4. I need _to_ buy some marshmallows for the campout.

5. Help me! This box is _too_ heavy for one person to carry.

6. We need _to_ carry the box to the backyard.

7. Look! Katy is _too_ short to reach the latch on the gate.

8. Get a ladder _to_ stand on.

9. I'll need the ladder, _too_.

Page 37

Marshmallow Roast

> Homophones are words that sound the same but are spelled differently and have different meanings.
>
> *I hear something.* hear = to listen to a sound
> *Stay here, and I'll look.* here = a place

Choose the correct homophone for each sentence. You may have to look up the meaning of some words in the dictionary.

When I _sent_ (scent, sent) my invitations, I asked everyone to bring something _for_ (for, four) our campout. When the _blue_ (blew, blue) sky turned gray, the clouds covered the _sun_ (sun, son), but it didn't rain.

We put bales of _hay_ (hey, hay) around the fire so we could sing camp songs together. My aunt _sent_ (sent, scent) some special chocolate from San Francisco for our s'mores. Mom thought it would be better to _grate_ (grate, great) the chocolate. Her idea did not turn out _great_ (grate, great). The chocolate melted and fell all over.

The best part of the night was when a _doe_ (dough, doe) walked through the woods with four other _deer_ (dear, deer).

Page 38

One Plus One Equals One

> Sometimes two words are joined together to make one new word. The new word is called a compound word.
>
> **cow + boy = cowboy**

Look at the words and pictures below. Add the words together and write the new word on the line.

bird + house =	_birdhouse_
horse + shoe =	_horseshoe_
pan + cake =	_pancake_
sun + flower =	_sunflower_
rain + coat =	_raincoat_

Try This Think of as many compound words as you can. Write down the different parts of each word, just like the ones above.

_____ + _____ = _____

Page 39

112

1-56822-908-9 *Building Grammar*

Fun on a Zoofari!

Compound words are two words joined together to make a new word.

foot + ball = football

Fill in the things we will need for our Zoofari. Use two words from the Word Bank to help you put together a compound word for each sentence.

1. Take a **flashlight** to see where you are walking at night.
2. Buy a **notebook** and a pencil to write about the animals.
3. Bring **sunflower** seeds to feed the birds.
4. The **weatherman** said it might rain, so let's take an umbrella.
5. We should also pack a **raincoat**.
6. We will buy a train ticket at the **railroad** office.
7. I will bring some **watermelon** and canteloupe.
8. Could you bring some **popcorn** without any salt?

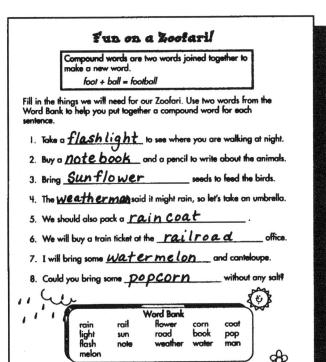

Word Bank				
rain	rail	flower	corn	coat
light	sun	road	book	pop
flash	note	weather	water	man
melon				

Page 40

Pow! Ouch! Yikes!

The sound of some words make you think of their meaning.
swish
buzz

Draw a line from each sentence to the correct picture.

1. What goes brring-brring?
2. What goes drip-drip?
3. What goes bang-bang?
4. What goes honk-honk?
5. What goes toot-toot?
6. What goes boom-boom?

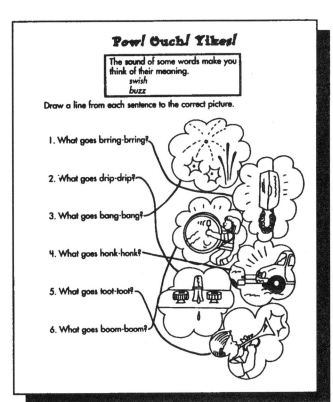

Page 41

Harmony Farm

The sound of some words make you think of their meaning.
swish
buzz

Look at these pictures from Harmony Farm. Use the Word Bank to write the correct sound word on the line.

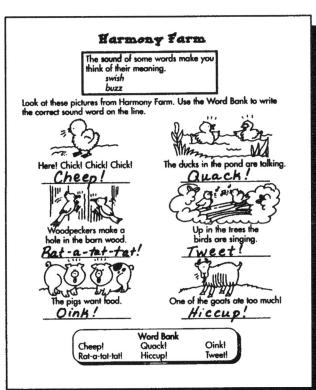

Here! Chick! Chick! Chick!
Cheep!

The ducks in the pond are talking.
Quack!

Woodpeckers make a hole in the barn wood.
Rat-a-tat-tat!

Up in the trees the birds are singing.
Tweet!

The pigs want food.
Oink!

One of the goats ate too much!
Hiccup!

Word Bank		
Cheep!	Quack!	Oink!
Rat-a-tat-tat!	Hiccup!	Tweet!

Page 42

More Books, Take a Look

Rhyming words are words that end with the same sound. Say these rhyming words out loud. Can you hear the rhyme?
box fox hat mat
corn horn dog frog

Circle all the book titles that rhyme. Then write the rhyming words from each title on the line.

1. *Kitten Can* _____
2. *Rat-a-Tat, Pitter-Pat* — **Rat, Tat, Pat**
3. *Hop on Pop* — **Hop, Pop**
4. *Like Jake and Me* _____
5. *Whose Shoe?* — **Whose, Shoe**
6. *Amelia Bedelia* — **Amelia, Bedelia**
7. *Hunches in Bunches* — **Hunches, Bunches**
8. *Aunt Flossie's Hats* _____
9. *Is Your Mama a Llama?* — **Mama, Llama**
10. *Sheep in a Jeep* — **Sheep, Jeep**

Try This Make up some rhyming book titles of your own.

Page 43

1-56822-908-9 *Building Grammar*

Should We Play?

Rhyming words are words that end with the same sound. Use your ears to hear the rhyme.

game, name
rover, over

Underline the rhyming words in each jump-rope rhyme.
Hint: It helps if you say them out loud.

Red Rover, Red <u>Rover</u>
Turn the jump rope <u>over</u>.
Faster and <u>slower</u>,
Higher and <u>lower</u>,
Let's speed up the <u>game</u>,
I'll shout out a <u>name</u>.

Baby, Baby in the tub,
Mama forgot to put in the plug.
Oh, what a shame!
Oh, what a pain!
There goes Baby down the <u>drain</u>!

Try This Make up a jump rope rhyme of your own. Here are some rhyming words to get started with, or choose your own.
| ring | itsy | fox | trip | hat | coat |
| ding | bitsy | box | slip | sat | boat |

Page 44

The Midnight Writer

There are lots of silly words. Some come from other languages or people's names. Many silly words are just made up.

hoity-toity

Read the mysterious letter Sue found under her pillow. Underline all the silly words. Hint: There are 5.

Dear Friend,

When you and your friends were walking <u>helter-skelter</u> in the woods, someone was watching you. Does that give you the <u>heebie-jeebies</u>?

I bet you are thinking, "Who could it be?" <u>Jeepers-creepers</u>! Do you think someone is looking for you? Or is it just one of your friends watching you?

Whoever or whatever, it left some footprints. Interested? If so, meet me for a <u>chitchat</u>.

A <u>roly-poly</u> friend

P.S. Bring puppy food and a leash.

Try This Can you solve the mystery? Who or what is following Sue?
Look up some other silly words in books or dictionaries or make up some of your own. Write a story or letter using some fun, made-up words.

Page 45

Mathantics

Numbers can be written many different ways. One way is to write a number as a word.
1 = one   2 = two   3 = three

Find the answers to these problems. Write your answers as words.

1. To ride on a seasaw you need **one** friend.

2. The **three** bears had a visit from Goldilocks.

3. If two friends sit at a table and three more sit down, there will be **five** at the table.

4. The number word that comes after eight and before ten is **nine** .

5. A car has **four** wheels.

6. Katie brought 3 pieces of gum. Jennifer brought 4 pieces. How many people can have gum? **seven**

7. There is only one chair at the table. How many people can sit at the table? **one**

8. For our game, we need 2 people to hold the jumprope and 2 people to jump. How many do we need for our game? **four**

Try This Use dice to play "Roll and Write." Roll the dice (you may also use one die) and write the numbers as words.

Page 46

First Place!

Sometimes we need to use special number words to show how people or things are related to each other. If someone won a race you would say:

Danny came in first.

The word *first* is called an ordinal number. The ordinal numbers are: **first, second, third, fourth, fifth, sixth, seventh, eighth, ninth,** and **tenth.**

Look at the picture below. Write the correct ordinal number next to each racer's picture.

1. is **third**
2. is **sixth**
3. is **tenth**
4. is **second**
5. is **first**

Page 47

1-56822-908-9 *Building Grammar*

Crazy Crayons

Color words help to tell about people, places, and things.

Dan is wearing a purple hat.
The flag is red, white, and blue.

Solve these color riddles.

green   red   white   orange   brown   yellow   blue   black   purple

The color of the stars on the American flag is __white__ .

A chalkboard can be the same color as grass, __green__ .

A gingerbread man is __brown__ .

An apple can be green, yellow, or __red__ .

The sun is __yellow__ .

The sky is __blue__ .

A car has __black__ tires.

A plum is red or __purple__ .

Pumpkins are __orange__

Try This Close your eyes and choose 20 crayons. Open your eyes and write a list of the colors you have in ABC order.

Page 48

Whose Smelly Sneakers?

An **adjective** is a word that describes a noun. Adjectives can tell about nouns by color, number, shape, size, feel, and smell.

The *small yellow* and *white* tennis shoes are Mary's.

Color each pair of tennis shoes to match the color word(s) that describes them. Then, underline the word(s) that tells about the shape, size, feel, or smell of each pair.

 1. Jimmy's yellow sneakers are <u>very long</u>.

 2. Jenny's purple tennis shoes have a <u>square</u> toe.

 3. Antonio's red and white striped sneakers have <u>short</u> laces.

 4. Yoshi's blue sneakers are <u>too small</u> for her.

 5. Missy's green tennis shoes are the <u>smallest</u> ones in our class.

6. These orange sneakers are <u>wet</u> and <u>smelly</u>.

Page 49

This Is My House

Adjectives can tell about things by size, shape, color, or number.

blue book	little boy
three poodles	square box

Help Carl finish these sentences that tell about his house. Use words that describe by color, size, shape, or number.

Some answers will vary.

1. I live in a _____ house. (color)

2. It is a _____ house. (size)

3. There are __five__ windows in my house. (number)

4. There are _____ violets and _____ roses growing in my yard. (color)

5. My front door has a __diamond__ window in it. (shape)

6. I have a very _____ driveway. (size)

7. I have __one__ pet(s). (number)

8. It is a __white__ rabbit. (color)

Try This Draw a picture of your house. Put in as many details as you can. Then write some sentences that describe your house.

Page 50

I'm Reading!

Adjectives tell more about nouns.

Robert is a nice boy.	*Nice tells more about Robert.*
We go to the school library on Tuesdays.	*School tells about the library.*
I like to read joke and riddle books.	*Joke and riddle tell more about books.*

Look at the list of books. Circle the word in each book title that tells more about the person, place, or thing. On the line, write whether the adjective tells more about a person or an animal, a place, or a thing.

(Silly) Sally   __person__

(Green) Eggs and Ham   __thing__

(Little) Bear   __animal__

The (Surprise) Party   __thing__

The (Snowy) Day   __thing__

Alexander and the (Wind-up) Mouse   __animal__

Try This Make up some book titles of your own with words that tell more about people, places, or things.

Page 51

1-56822-908-9 *Building Grammar*

Cloudy or Sunny?

> Some adjectives tell what the weather is like today or what it might be like tomorrow.
> *Today is cloudy.*

Pretend you are the weather person. Look at the pictures below. Write two adjectives from the Word Bank on the lines next to each picture.

 Sunny   Sizzling
hot   warm

 rainy, cloudy,
Stormy, gray,
windy

 Snowy   freezing
icy   cold

Word Bank

sunny	rainy	cloudy	hot	snowy
sizzling	stormy	gray	warm	icy
windy	foggy	freezing	cold	

Page 52

Who's Faster?

> Adjectives that compare two things end in er.
> *It's cold inside.*
> *It is colder outside than inside.*

Use the Word Bank to write a comparing word in the blank of each sentence below. Then answer the question with a sentence.

Answers may vary slightly.

Word Bank

colder	slower	darker	faster	longer
smaller	bigger	taller	warmer	

1. Which is __colder__, Alaska or Hawaii?
   Alaska is colder than Hawaii.
2. What's __darker__, night or day?
   Night is darker than day.
3. Is a turtle __faster__ than a rabbit?
   No, a turtle is slower than a rabbit.
4. Who is __bigger__, an ant or an alligator?
   An alligator is bigger than an ant.
5. Is Africa __warmer__ than the North Pole?
   Africa is warmer than the North Pole.
6. Is your teacher __taller__ than you?
   My teacher is taller than I am.

Page 53

Who's the Fastest?

> Adjectives that compare more than two things end in est.
> *Their houses are cold, but my house is the coldest.*
> *My bicycle is the largest of all my toys.*

Look at the picture below. Use the Word Bank to complete the sentences with the correct est comparing word. Some adjectives won't be used.

Word Bank

tallest	coldest	fastest	biggest	smallest
widest	slowest	kindest	longest	

1. The roadrunner is the __fastest__ runner. He won the race.
2. Turtle is the __slowest__ runner. He came in last.
3. With her cage full of ice, the penguin is the __coldest__ racer.
4. Since the jaguar offered to carry the kangaroo, he may be the __kindest__ animal in the race.
5. The anteater is the runner with the __longest__ nose.
6. The __smallest__ runner is the mouse.

Page 54

Taller, Higher . . .

> Adjectives that compare usually end in er or est. When we compare two people, places, or things, we use er.
> *Tom is taller than Roberto.*
> When we compare three or more, we add est.
> *Samantha is the tallest of all the girls.*

Use the graph and the Word Bank to complete the sentences below.

Jenny   José   Maria   Dan

1. (Maria) is the __tallest__.
2. (Jenny) and (José) are __taller__ than (Dan).
3. (Jenny) is __shorter__ than (José).
4. (Dan) is the __shortest__.

Word Bank

taller	tallest	shorter	shortest

Page 55

1-56822-908-9 *Building Grammar*

As the Years Go By

> **Adjectives** that compare two people, places, or things usually end in **er**. Adjectives that compare three or more usually end in **est**.
>
> *Paige is faster.*
> *Paige is the fastest.*

Use the graph and the Word Bank to complete the sentences below.

Kyle	☆☆☆
Ashley	☆☆☽
Roberto	☆☆☆☆
Sara	☆☆☆☽
Mrs. Alton	☆☆☆☆☆☆☆☆☆☆☆☆☆

☆ = 2 years

1. Mrs. Alton is the __oldest__.
2. Ashley is the __youngest__.
3. Roberto is __older__ than Sara.
4. Kyle is __younger__ than Sara.

Word Bank
older   oldest   younger   youngest

Page 56

Where Do You Live?

> The describing words *a*, *an*, and *the* are called **articles**.
> **A** and **an** can mean any person or thing.
>   *I got a book.*
> Use *an* in front of words that start with vowels: *a, e, i, o,* and *u.*
>   *An Eskimo lives in an igloo.*
> **The** means a particular thing or things.
>   *I read the book that you read last week.*

Read each sentence and complete it by drawing a line to the correct description. Fill in the missing articles and finish each sentence.

1. I live where it is always cold, in a house that could melt.
   I am . . .

2. I pace back and forth, back and forth. Sometimes I pace so fast you can't see my stripes through the bars on . . .

3. I live in New York City. My house is so tall it reaches to the clouds. I live in a building with lots of other people . . .

4. My home is where it gets very hot. Sometimes my only neighbors are lizards.
   I live on . . .
   I am . . .

__a__ cage in __the__ zoo.

__an__ Eskimo in __an__ igloo.

__a__ reservation.
__a__ Navajo.

in __an__ apartment on __the__ thirtieth floor.

Page 57

Describing Words

> **Adverbs** are words that tell more about verbs. They tell **when**, **where**, or **how** an action takes place.
>
> *We eat indoors.*
> Indoors tells more about **where** we eat.
> *The race started late.*
> Late tells **when** the race started.
> *Runners work hard.*
> Hard tells **how** runners work.

Underline each adverb you find in the sentences below.

1. Grandma snores <u>loudly</u>.
2. Jamie leaves <u>tomorrow</u>.
3. Amy always sits <u>here</u>.
4. The baby eats <u>often</u>.
5. Animals are <u>nearby</u>.
6. My pony ran <u>quickly</u>.
7. Rafael drove <u>slowly</u>.
8. I will go to school <u>later</u>.

Page 58

To the Fair

> **Adverbs** tell more about verbs. They can tell **when**, **where**, or **how** an action takes place.
>
> *Robbie rode today. (when)*
> *Robbie rode outdoors. (where)*
> *Robbie rode slowly. (how)*

Read the following story. Underline each adverb that you find. Hint: there are 14 adverbs.

Grandma took me to the fair <u>yesterday</u>. We drove <u>slowly</u> in her car. Grandma honked her horn <u>loudly</u>. We drove <u>far away</u>.

The pigs at the fair squealed <u>often</u>. The cows mooed <u>sadly</u>. Horses pranced <u>nearby</u>. They danced <u>gracefully</u>.

I laughed <u>cheerfully</u> with the clowns. <u>Nearby</u>, Grandma won first place in the apple pie competition. She <u>happily</u> accepted the blue ribbon.

On the drive home, I fell asleep <u>quickly</u>. Grandma laid my head <u>gently</u> in her lap. When we got home, she <u>tenderly</u> put me to bed. We had an exciting day!

Try This   Write a story about a trip you took. Make sure to use lots of adverbs.

Page 59

1-56822-908-9 *Building Grammar*

How in the World?

> Adverbs tell more about verbs. They can tell when, where, or how an action takes place.
>
> I walked *today*. (when)
> I walked *nearby*. (where)
> I walked *quickly*. (how)

Write when, where, or how on the line to show what each adverb tells.

1. I run sometimes. — *when*
2. Meredith walks swiftly. — *how*
3. My dog drinks outside. — *where*
4. Dan bikes weekly. — *when*
5. The car drove slowly. — *how*
6. My purse is there. — *where*
7. Joel plays happily. — *how*
8. Kate dives next. — *when*
9. Jacob reads inside. — *where*
10. I leap gracefully. — *how*

Page 60

When, Where, and How?

> Adverbs tell more about verbs. They help tell when, where, or how an action takes place.
>
> I eat *often*. (when)
> I eat *nearby*. (where)
> I eat *quickly*. (how)

Finish these sentences with adverbs. Your adverb must answer the question word in parentheses.

Answers will vary.

1. I skipped _____ down the lane. (how)
2. John walked his dog _____ . (where)
3. I will _____ brush my teeth. (when)
4. My family eats dinner _____ . (how)
5. Lucy dances _____ . (how)
6. We go to the movies _____ . (when)
7. Karen goes jogging _____ . (when)
8. I will walk _____ . (where)

Page 61

Monopoly Mania

> A pronoun takes the place of a noun. Subject pronouns take the place of the subject in a sentence.
>
> *Roberto likes to play Monopoly.*
> *He likes to play Monopoly.*

Replace each bold noun with the correct subject pronoun. Choose from these subject pronouns: I, you, he, she, it, we, they. Write it on the line.

1. **Roberto** opens the Monopoly board. *he*
2. **Julia** chooses the racing car as her playing piece. *she*
3. **Maria** wants to be the banker. Maria likes math. *she*
4. **Roberto and Michael** decide to take care of the real estate. *They*
5. **Maria, Michael, Julia, and Roberto** roll the dice to see who goes first. *they*
6. **Julia** rolls the highest number and starts the game. *she*
7. **Roberto** rolls seven and goes to jail. *he*
8. **Roberto** rolls three times before he rolls doubles and gets out of jail. *he*
9. "Let's count our money to see who won," **Michael** says. *he*
10. "Maria wins," **Roberto** says. "She has the most money." *he*

Page 62

Lunch at the Creature Café

> Pronouns take the place of nouns.
>
> *Katie and I = we*
> *Katie, Jenny, and Sean = they*
> *lasagna = it*

Katie and Jenny made a date to meet at the Creature Café for lunch. Underline all the subject pronouns in Jenny's journal entry about their meal. Pronouns: I, you, he, she, it, we, they.

Saturday, January 27

Katie and <u>I</u> met at the Creature Café. <u>We</u> looked at the menu. <u>It</u> had funny creature names for the food. <u>We</u> were served Sizzling Snake Soup. There were no snakes. It was really made with noodles. <u>We</u> ate Leapin' Lizard Lasagna. <u>It</u> was yummy. For dessert, <u>we</u> had Penguin Popsicles. After <u>we</u> ate lunch, <u>we</u> hugged. <u>We</u> said we would meet for lunch next month. <u>I</u> waved goodbye as my friend Katie drove away.

Try This Write a journal entry of what happened today at lunch.

Page 63

Published by Instructional fair. Copyright protected.

1-56822-908-9 *Building Grammar*

It Is Missing

A pronoun takes the place of a noun (person, place, or thing).
person = I, you, he, she, we, they
thing or place = it

Mary hid under the table.
She hid under it.

Write the correct pronoun on the line after each word in bold type to take the place of each noun.

King Riggle and His Missing Crown

Once upon a time in the land of Woggles, there was a king named Riggle. **King Riggle** _he_ loved to wear his crown. **King Riggle** _he_ even wore the **crown** _it_ to bed. The only time he took the crown off was when he ate his **lunch** _it_ . That was because **the crown** _it_ always fell into his mashed potatoes.

One day the king's crown was missing.
"**The Woggles** _they_ must find my crown!" King Riggle said.

All of the Woggles looked up and looked down the land. But the **Woggles** _they_ did not find the king's crown. The gardener didn't find the **crown** _it_ . The **butler** _he_ who carried King Riggle's food to the table didn't find **the crown** _it_ . However, the crown was found in the kitchen. Can you guess who found **the crown** _it_ and where?

For You

Object pronouns replace the object of the sentence. They are usually in the last part of the sentence. They are: me, you, her, him, them, us, and it.

Molly gave the game to us.
I wrote a note to her.

Replace each object in the sentences below with an object pronoun. Write the pronoun on the line after each sentence. Remember, the object pronouns are: me, you, her, him, them, us, and it.

1. Kevin gave Robert a candy bar.   _him_
2. I rode on the bus.   _it_
3. Laurie tossed the ball to Becky.   _her_
4. Sharon ate the apple.   _it_
5. Roberto cheered for Sue and Dan.   _them_
6. Janelle drove David and me to the fair.   _us_
7. I walked Mario to school.   _him_
8. Mrs. Walker gave my class a treat.   _us_

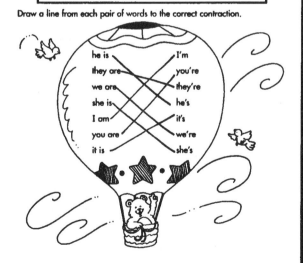

We're Together

Some words like is and are can be put together with other words to make contractions. The i of *is* or the a of *are* is dropped and added to a pronoun. They are connected by an apostrophe (').
    it + is = it's   you + are = you're
Remember: in a contraction, the whole first word is still there.

Draw a line from each pair of words to the correct contraction.

he is   I'm
they are   you're
we are   they're
she is   he's
I am   it's
you are   we're
it is   she's

We'll Work Together

A pronoun and the word will can be put together to make a shorter word called a contraction. An apostrophe (') takes the place of any letters left out.

Singular	Plural
I will = I'll	we will = we'll
you will = you'll	they will = they'll
he will = he'll	

I will help Mary study.
I'll help Mary study.

Make the following letter shorter by writing a contraction on the line after each set of words in bold type.

Dear Mr. Woods,
   Our class will help in the library. Here is the list of what **we will** _We'll_ do:
      Michelle **will** _She'll_ organize the work crew schedule.
      Sara and Henry **will** _They'll_ pick up any trash.
      We will _We'll_ borrow your big broom to sweep the sidewalks.
      Mario volunteered. **He will** _He'll_ get big garbage bags.
      Ronnie, Joy, and Katy **will** _They'll_ help keep birds away from the construction area.
      I will _I'll_ let the work crews leave class 15 minutes early for recess.
      You will _You'll_ be happy with our work.
                              Sincerely,
                              Mrs. Alton

1-56822-908-9 *Building Grammar*

Do not, Did not

A verb and the word **not** can be put together to make a shorter word called a **contraction**. An apostrophe (') takes the place of any letters left out.

is not = isn't   do not = don't
did not = didn't   are not = aren't

Write the contractions that can replace some of the words in Mary's letter to her friend. Write them above the old words.

Dear Jimmy,
     isn't   *didn't*
    Disneyland is not far from the beach. We did not ride a
                        didn't
train to Disneyland. We drove our car. Disneyland did not open
until 9 o'clock.
     didn't
    We did not agree on what to do first. Finally, we began
             didn't
our visit in Fantasyland. We did not want to miss any fun. We
                I'm   *couldn't*
stayed until midnight. It was so much fun! I am sorry you could
not go with us. If we take this trip again, my mother promised
    you're   *You'll*   *Isn't*
that you are not staying at home. You will come with us! Is not
that exciting?

                Your friend,

                Mary

Page 68

Where's My Stuff?

A verb and the word **not** can be put together to make a shorter word called a **contraction**. An apostrophe (') takes the place of any letters left out.

did not = didn't

Greg had so many things in his backpack that it broke and everything spilled out. His friends were walking behind him. What did each friend find? Write the two words on the lines that make up each contraction. Then write what Greg's friend's found on the answer line.

1. "Who found my package with something I chew at recess?" asked Greg.
    "I didn't (**did not**) find your gum, but I found something you write with on paper," said Jamie.
    Answer: **pencil**

2. "I don't (**do not**) have my compass. Who has it?" asked Greg.
    "I can't (**can not**) find north or south, but I can get rid of wrong answers," said Emily.
    Answer: **eraser**

3. "My yo-yo isn't (**is not**) in my backpack," said Greg.
    "I don't (**do not**) have it," said Jerry, "but I have something else to use at recess. There are at least 50 round balls. Some are clear. Some look like cats' eyes. Others are solid colors and stripes."
    Answer: **marbles**

Page 69

Morning Message

A **sentence** is a group of words that tells a complete idea about someone or something.

The girls are coming home. (sentence)
The girls home (not a sentence)

Mrs. Alton wrote a morning message to her class on the chalkboard. Some of her sentences don't make sense. Underline the sentences that don't tell a complete idea.

Today is Tuesday. <u>It is the day after.</u> This morning I will read a book. <u>Its title is.</u> The P.E. teacher will teach us to play soccer. <u>Soccer is.</u>

We will make a graph. <u>Before we go home.</u> You can check out three books.

Try This Can you fix the morning message for Mrs. Alton by putting in words to make her sentences complete?

Page 70

The Creature Café

A **sentence** is a group of words that tells a complete thought or idea.

John and Melanie eat red and green apples.(sentence)
eat red and green apples (not a sentence)

Find and underline the complete sentences in The Creature Café's Menu.

The Creature Café

Penguin Pizza
<u>The pizza is made with white cheese and black olives.</u>
No Spaghetti Sauce

Cheetah Cheese Sandwich
Melted yellow cheese on toasted white bread.
<u>After you eat this sandwich, you'll run like a cheetah.</u>

Soups
Owl Onion
<u>An owl would rather gulp it up than snooze.</u>

Pig n' Potato
Little chunks of ham and potato. Warm and creamy.

Salads
Goat Cheese
<u>Plain lettuce and tomato are sprinkled with goat cheese.</u>

Coyote Caesar
<u>You'll howl when you taste this special dressing.</u>

Drinks
Raccoon's Raspberry Tea
<u>Even with a mask, you can taste the sweet raspberries in this tea.</u>

Lion Lemonade
<u>This golden yellow juice roars with sweetness.</u>

Page 71

1-56822-908-9 *Building Grammar*

All Mixed Up

The order of the words in a sentence tells what the sentence means.

Sam the banana eats. (wrong)
The banana eats Sam. (wrong)
Sam eats the banana. (correct)

Draw a line from the picture to the sentence that makes sense.

1. The bag fell out of Sam's sandwich.
   Sam's sandwich fell out of the bag.

2. The dog ran after the ball.
   The ball ran after the dog.

3. Sam's candy bar melted the sun.
   The sun melted Sam's candy bar.

Try This Draw a silly picture of a mixed-up sentence.

Page 72

More Mix-Ups

The order of the words in a sentence tells what the sentence means.

The cow milks the man. (wrong)
The man milks the cow. (right)

Draw a line from the picture to the sentence that makes sense.

1. Mary ate the cookies.
   The cookies ate Mary.

2. My skin burned the sun.
   The sun burned my skin.

3. The bunny ate the carrots.
   The carrots ate the bunny.

Page 73

Bulletin Board Mix-Up

A sentence always starts with a **capital letter**.

<u>The</u> zebra lost its stripes.
<u>He</u> found them in the leopard's cage.

Circle the words on the "Star of the Week" board that need capital letters.

Star of the Week

Maria is tall.
she has black hair.

our star has a dog.
his name is Cleo.

disneyworld is her favorite place.
She likes Toon Town.

she likes to read books.

Try This Make a "Star of the Week" board for yourself. How many are in your family? What's your favorite food? Make sure all your sentences start with a capital letter and end with a period.

Page 74

My First Day

Telling sentences end with a period. Periods are like stop signs. They tell you when a sentence ends.

The sentence ends here.

Fix these sentences. Some need a period. Some need more words and a period. The missing words are in the Word Bank.

Word Bank		
pizza	Mrs. Hill	class
friends	soccer	bus

1. I like school.
2. My teacher's name is **Mrs. Hill.**
3. I have three **friends.**
4. At recess, we play **soccer.**
5. On Monday, we have music **class.**
6. My favorite food for lunch is **pizza.**
7. We are learning addition in math class.
8. I ride the **bus** to school.

Try This Write your own story about school. Then give it to a friend to read. Did you remember all the periods?

Page 75

1-56822-908-9 *Building Grammar*

Snack Time

A telling sentence tells something. It ends with a period.
Ice cream is cold.

Read each label and underline the telling sentences for each snack.

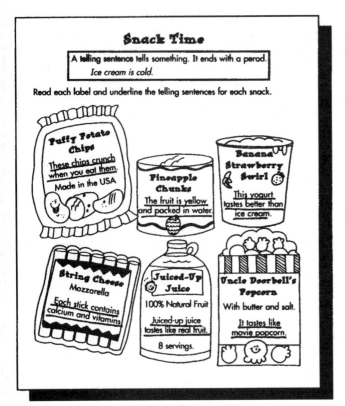

Puffy Potato Chips
These chips crunch when you eat them.
Made in the USA

Pineapple Chunks
The fruit is yellow and packed in water.

Banana Strawberry Swirl
This yogurt tastes better than ice cream.

String Cheese
Mozzarella
Each stick contains calcium and vitamins

Juiced-Up Juice
100% Natural Fruit
Juiced-up juice tastes like real fruit.
8 servings.

Uncle Doorbell's Popcorn
With butter and salt.
It tastes like movie popcorn.

Page 76

Rollin' at Recess

A telling sentence tells about someone or something.
A telling sentence starts with a capital and ends with a period.
Molly is playing jacks.

Finish these telling sentences about some kids at recess. All the words you will need are in the Word Bank. The picture clues will help you.

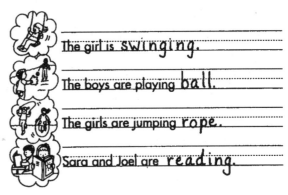

The girl is swinging.

The boys are playing ball.

The girls are jumping rope.

Sara and Joel are reading.

Word Bank
ball   swinging   reading   rope

Page 77

Marble Mania

An asking sentence asks a question. It always begins with a capital letter and ends with a question mark.
What did you bring for lunch today?

Write asking sentences to go with the picture below. Use the Word Bank for help.

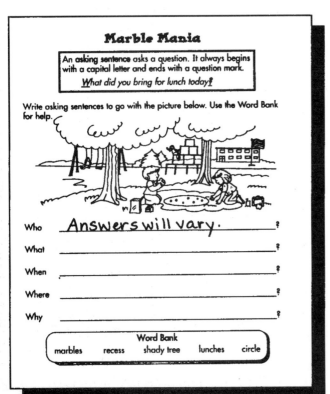

Who   Answers will vary.   ?
What   _____ ?
When   _____ ?
Where _____ ?
Why   _____ ?

Word Bank
marbles   recess   shady tree   lunches   circle

Page 78

Whom Do I Ask?

An asking sentence asks a question about something or someone. It always ends with a question mark.
Who will help me carry this heavy box?

Underline each asking sentence. Write answers from the Word Bank in the blanks.

1. I need a book to read. Who can help me find one?
   The **librarian** can help you find a book.
2. I cut my knee. Who can help me?
   The **nurse** can help you.
3. Who can teach me how to read?
   Your **teacher** will help you learn to read.
4. Who can help me clean up this milk?
   The **janitor** will bring his mop.
5. Who can teach me to play the violin?
   The **music teacher** knows how to play.
6. Who can show me how to draw a picture of a zebra?
   The **art teacher** can show you how to draw a zebra.

Word Bank
nurse   librarian   teacher   janitor
music teacher   art teacher

Page 79

1-56822-908-9 *Building Grammar*

I Have a Secret

Telling sentences tell something. They end with a period(.).

I have a secret.

Asking sentences ask a question. They end with a question mark(?).

Do you want to know what it is?

Put a period at the end of each telling sentence. Put a question mark at the end of each asking sentence.

1. I'll tell you.
2. Do you promise not to tell anyone?
3. Tomorrow is my birthday.
4. Can you guess what I'm making for the class?
5. I am baking cupcakes.
6. Do you like chocolate or vanilla frosting?
7. What kind of ice cream do you like?
8. I think I know your answer.
9. Should I ask Mrs. Alton if we can celebrate after math?

Page 80

Hannah Hippo's Trip

An asking sentence asks a question. It ends with a ?

Where is Hannah Hippo going?

A telling sentence tells something. It ends with a .

Hannah is going to Florida.

Decide if each sentence is asking or telling. Then put the correct punctuation at the end of each sentence.

Hannah Hippo wants to go on a trip.

Should she ride the bus or take the train?

Hannah Hippo finally finds a jumbo jet.

Hannah lands in Florida.

Where is Auntie?

Will Auntie get there in time to pick up Hannah?

Try This Finish the story of Hannah Hippo's trip with asking and telling sentences.

Page 81

Animal Jeopardy

A telling sentence can be changed to an asking sentence.

Horses eat grass.
What do horses eat?

Change the telling sentences below to asking sentences. Remember the question mark (?) at the end of your asking sentence. The first one has been done for you.

1. A giraffe can eat leaves on tall trees.

   <u>What can a giraffe eat?</u>

2. Monkeys eat bananas.

   <u>What do monkeys eat?</u>

3. Zebras look like horses with stripes.

   <u>What do zebras look like?</u>

4. Elephants are the biggest animals at the zoo.

   <u>What are the biggest animals at the zoo?</u>

5. Panda bears are from China.

   <u>Where are panda bears from?</u>

6. Turtles live in shells.

   <u>Where do turtles live?</u>

Page 82

Sh-h-h-! Be Quiet.

Some sentences show strong feeling or surprise. They end with an exclamation point(!).

Its teeth are sharp!

Other sentences give a command or make a request. They end with a period(.).

Sit down in your seat.

If the sentence tells something exciting, put an exclamation mark (!) at the end. If it tells you to do something, put a period (.) at the end.

1. Oh no, the hungry lion is missing!
2. Lock the gate so the others won't escape.
3. His teeth are so sharp!
4. Follow his tracks.
5. Look, he's back!
6. Find the key to his cage.
7. Open the door.
8. Put food in his cage.
9. Wow, that was close!

Page 83

Published by Instructional fair. Copyright protected.

1-56822-908-9 *Building Grammar*

Where in the World?

A sentence that gives a command or makes a request ends with
a period. It usually tells you to do something.

Please shut the door.

Maria is telling her friend Emily how to get to her house. Finish the
command sentences using the map to Maria's house.

Word Bank

school	Grass	Road	courts
Sky	park	Lake	Lucy

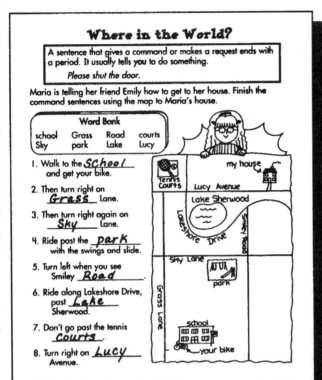

1. Walk to the *school*
   and get your bike.

2. Then turn right on
   Grass Lane.

3. Then turn right again on
   Sky Lane.

4. Ride past the *park*
   with the swings and slide.

5. Turn left when you see
   Smiley *Road* .

6. Ride along Lakeshore Drive,
   past *Lake*
   Sherwood.

7. Don't go past the tennis
   courts .

8. Turn right on *Lucy*
   Avenue.

Page 84

.?!

There are four kinds of sentences.
   Declarative (.)—tells something
      I helped the librarian put away books.
   Interrogative (?)—asks a question
      *Do you know how many books are in our
      library?*
   Exclamatory (!)—makes a strong, surprised, or angry
      statement
      Wow, that box of books is heavy!
   Imperative (.)—gives a command or makes a request
      Help carry some of these boxes.

Write the name of the kind of sentence on the line after each sentence.
Then, put in the punctuation that belongs with each sentence.

1. Hooray, it's finally here! *exclamatory*

2. Our new library will open in two more days. *declarative*

3. Bring your parents to the dedication on Thursday. *imperative*

4. Do you know what time the dedication starts? *interrogative*

5. It begins at ten o'clock. *declarative*

6. Tell them to be here early to get a good seat. *imperative*

7. Does the library look fantastic? *interrogative*

8. We should all be proud. *declarative*

9. I'm so excited! *exclamatory*

Page 85

Pet Shop

Every sentence ends with a punctuation mark. Statements,
commands, or requests end with a period. Questions end
with a question mark. Sentences with strong feeling or
emotion end with an exclamation mark.

   I like to read.
   Please pass the noodles.
   Do you understand?
   We won!

Put the correct punctuation mark at the end of each sentence.

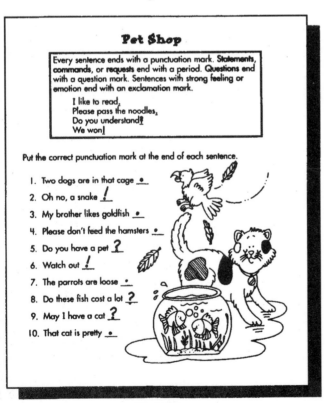

1. Two dogs are in that cage .

2. Oh no, a snake !

3. My brother likes goldfish .

4. Please don't feed the hamsters .

5. Do you have a pet ?

6. Watch out !

7. The parrots are loose .

8. Do these fish cost a lot ?

9. May I have a cat ?

10. That cat is pretty .

Page 86

Goodnight .?!

Sentences must have proper punctuation marks at the end.
Periods end sentences that make statements.
   Someone is at my door.
Question marks end sentences that ask questions.
   Who is at my door?
Exclamation marks end sentences that show strong feeling
or emotion.
   When I saw the bear, I fainted!

Maria's mother is trying to get the kids at the campout to go to sleep.
Place the correct punctuation mark on the line at the end of each sentence.

11:00 P.M.   Maria's mother walks outside, smiling .
   "Do you kids know what time it is ?
   It's time for lights out . "

11:15 P.M.   Maria's mother walks outside, frowning .
   "Second warning . or !
   You may still whisper .
   Do you know how to whisper ? .

11:30 P.M.   Maria's mother and father walk out together .
   They are both frowning .
   "This is your third warning . or !
   No more whispering or giggling .
   Close your eyes .
   You have an early soccer game tomorrow .
   Get to sleep . "

12:00 A.M.   Maria's father comes out alone .
   He's rubbing his head .
   "The next person I hear goes home .
   Goodnight . or "
   !

Page 87

1-56822-908-9 *Building Grammar*

Together at Last

Two sentences can be joined together if their ideas are alike. When you join sentences, add and, or, or but.
Mary hugs her sister. + *Mary leaves.*
Mary hugs her sister and leaves.

See if you can combine these pairs of sentences into one sentence. Write the new sentence on the line.

1. Jerry has five balls. + Jerry has two bats.

Jerry has five balls and two bats.

2. Sara baked cookies. + Sara baked muffins.

Sara baked cookies and muffins.

3. The dog ran. + The dog barked.

The dog ran and barked.

4. My mom loves books. + My mom loves pictures.

My mom loves books and pictures.

Page 88

Let's Get Together

Join two sentences if their ideas are similar by using and, or, or but.
Betsy tickles the baby. + *Betsy giggles.*
Betsy tickles the baby and giggles.

Combine each pair of sentences into one sentence. Write the new sentence on the line.

1. Alyson jumped down. + Alyson tripped.

Alyson jumped down and tripped.

2. The squirrel grabbed the nut. + The squirrel ran.

The squirrel grabbed the nut and ran.

3. My dad mows the lawn. + My dad clips the hedges.

My dad mows the lawn and clips the hedges.

4. I love to read books. + I love to read magazines.

I love to read books and magazines.

Page 89

The I's Have It

When you talk about yourself, you use the word I. You are important, so I is always capitalized. Remember, when I stands alone, it is always capitalized.

I had fun at recess.
Jack and I played on the swings.

It's recess. Your friend wrote you a secret note. To find out what he said, fill in the blanks with either a capital *I* or a small *i*.

_I_ have a surpr_i_se for us after school. Could you come to my house? _I_ t will be fun! You and _I_ could make cook_i_es. _I_ like to bake. Do you?

_I_ will call my mother at recess. She w_i_ll pick us up after school. _I_ think she might take us to get _i_ce-cream cones too. _I_ like Cook_i_es and Cream. What _i_ce-cream flavor do you l_i_ke best?

Later, _I_ think we will play ball. _I_ have a box full of bats, balls, and gloves.

Please say yes. _I_ want you to be my friend.

Page 90

Logo Land

Special names of people and places are called proper nouns. They always begin with a capital letter.
Mr. Jones   Disneyland

Help Mr. Dibble, the city sign painter, fix the signs. Underline each word that needs a capital letter.

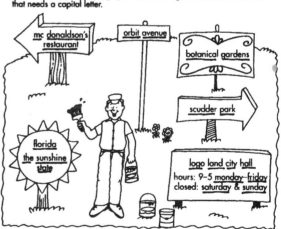

mc donaldson's restaurant

orbit avenue

botanical gardens

scudder park

florida the sunshine state

logo land city hall
hours: 9–5 monday–friday
closed: saturday & sunday

Try This Make your own sign for your school or town.

Page 91

1-56822-908-9 *Building Grammar*

What's Missing?

Names of specific people and places always begin with a capital letter. These are called **proper nouns.**

Patty is my best friend. (name of a person)
She lives in California. (name of a place)

This is a page from Kacie's phone book. She made some mistakes. She forgot the capitals for names and places. Can you help her fix them?

jenny simon
69 black beauty drive
aspen, colorado 81611

Jenny Simon
69 Black Beauty Drive
Aspen, Colorado 81611

aunt molly
562 compass circle
san diego, california 92101

Aunt Molly
562 Compass Circle
San Diego, California 92101

jeremy binner
8941 lakeshore drive
tempe, arizona 85280

Jeremy Binner
8941 Lakeshore Drive
Tempe, Arizona 85280

Try This Start your own address book. Get the names, addresses, and phone numbers of family and friends and put them in alphabetical order. Don't forget the capital letters.

Page 92

A Name? A Name!

The names of specific people and places begin with capital letters. These are called **proper nouns.**

George Washington
Portland, Oregon

Mrs. Poppins, the principal, has asked students at Pleasant Elementary School to suggest names for their new library. Circle each word below that needs a capital letter.

1. The library should be named the book market—Lisa

2. Name it babe ruth library—Jeremy

3. The library's new name should be the land of adventure. sara nagel

4. Let's name it the friendship library—jenny wagner

5. We could use the big apple new york city's nickname, for our library.
   Sean Carpenter

6. Libraries are places to be quiet and read. Let's name it quiet zone. Mike from mrs. alton's class

7. The pleasant elementary school library should be named after someone who writes books, such as louisa may alcott, beverly cleary, tomie de paola or shel silverstein.—Teresa

Page 93

Calendar Capers

Proper nouns include days of the week, months of the year, and special holidays. They always begin with a capital letter.

Thanksgiving is always on the last Thursday in November.

Using the Word Bank below, write the month at the top of the calendar. Fill in the missing days of the week. Ask your teacher to help you number the calendar for the current year. Write in the special holidays for the month.

December

Sunday	Monday	Tuesday	Wednesday	Thursday	Friday	Saturday
Holidays	will	vary:				
Christmas		Hanukkah				
New Year's Eve		Kwanza				

Word Bank

saturday   monday   thursday   sunday   wednesday
december   christmas   hanukkah   new year's eve
kwanza

Page 94

First, Last, and Important

Titles of books, movies, and TV shows are always capitalized. Capitalize the first, last, and important words in the title.

The Cat in the Hat
Alexander and the Terrible, Horrible, No Good, Very Bad Day

Circle the words in the titles that need capital letters.

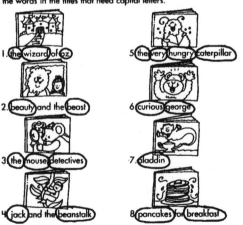

1. the wizard of oz

2. beauty and the beast

3. the mouse detectives

4. jack and the beanstalk

5. the very hungry caterpillar

6. curious george

7. aladdin

8. pancakes for breakfast

Page 95

1-56822-908-9 *Building Grammar*

I'm From . . .

Just like your name, the names of cities and states are **proper nouns** and must have capital letters. A comma goes between the city name and the state name.

Detroit, Michigan

First, write the name of your city and state below. Don't forget the capital letters and the comma.

Answers will vary.

Next, write the names of the following cities and states with capital letters and commas.

1. phoenix arizona   *Phoenix, Arizona*
2. fargo north dakota   *Fargo, North Dakota*
3. boise idaho   *Boise, Idaho*
4. buffalo new york   *Buffalo, New York*
5. macon georgia   *Macon, Georgia*
6. st. louis missouri   *St. Louis, Missouri*
7. san antonio texas   *San Antonio, Texas*
8. eureka california   *Eureka, California*

Page 96

Teeny, Weeny Calendar

Sometimes we **abbreviate** the names of the days of the week or the names of the months of the year. May, June, and July are very short and do not need to be abbreviated. Every **abbreviation** ends with a period.

Mon. = Monday   Jan. = January

Fit the days of the week on this teeny, weeny calendar. Pick your favorite month of the year; their abbreviations are listed for you in the Word Bank below.

Word Bank

Jan.	Mar.	May	June
Apr.	Sept.	Feb.	Dec.
Nov.	Oct.	July	Aug.

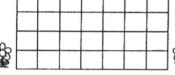

Will vary.

Sun.	Mon.	Tues.	Wed.	Thurs.	Fri.	Sat.

Try This   Design your own teeny, weeny pocket calendar.

Page 97

A Postcard Reminder

Commas set apart the names of a city and state.

I live in New York City, New York. (in sentences)

25 W. Fifth Ave.
New York City, New York (in addresses on letters)

A list with more than two people, places, or things also needs commas between each item in the list.

Please bring a pair of tennis shoes, a sleeping bag, a water bottle, and a snack.

The kids going to the campout got a postcard telling them what to bring. Put commas where they belong in the message and the address.

Molly,
You need to bring a sleeping bag, a toothbrush, a pillow, and a bag of chips.

Becky

Molly Sleepy
52 Brown St.
Seattle, WA 98101

Annie,
You're in charge of games. Bring backgammon, chess, checkers, and your fortune-telling cards.

Becky

Annie Awake
19 Green Grove Dr.
Seattle, WA 98101

Page 98

Get in Line!

When you have a list of three or more you must put **commas** between each item in the list.

I bought apples, oranges, peaches, and grapes.

Put commas where they belong in each sentence below.

1. Katie, Dan, and Bobby played together.
2. It rained on Wednesday, Thursday, and Friday.
3. I have been to Michigan, Ohio, Iowa, and New York.
4. Today we will study math, science, reading, and music.
5. I like to ski, skate, and sled in the winter.
6. My favorite foods are carrots, apples, cookies, and chips.
7. Sara needs her pencil, paper, crayons, and scissors.
8. Today we will read, draw, and listen to stories.

Page 99

127

Star Gazers

> **Quotation marks are used to show what people say.**
> *"I saw two shooting stars!" yelled Robert.*

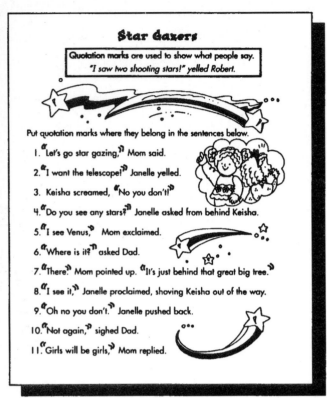

Put quotation marks where they belong in the sentences below.

1. "Let's go star gazing," Mom said.

2. "I want the telescope!" Janelle yelled.

3. Keisha screamed, "No you don't!"

4. "Do you see any stars?" Janelle asked from behind Keisha.

5. "I see Venus," Mom exclaimed.

6. "Where is it?" asked Dad.

7. "There." Mom pointed up. "It's just behind that great big tree."

8. "I see it," Janelle proclaimed, shoving Keisha out of the way.

9. "Oh no you don't." Janelle pushed back.

10. "Not again," sighed Dad.

11. "Girls will be girls," Mom replied.

Page 100

Are You Talking to Me?

> **Quotation marks are used to set off the exact words of a speaker.**
> *"Listen Mark," said John. "Did you hear that?"*

Put quotation marks around what Mrs. Poppins said and what the students said.

1. "I am here to get some ideas for our new library," Mrs. Poppins said.

2. "I'd like a skylight," said Jenny.

3. "H-m-m," said Mrs. Poppins. In her notebook she wrote what Jenny said.

4. "I think we need a corner with lots of big, fluffy pillows," Tim said.

5. "H-m-m," said Mrs. Poppins, and she wrote down what Tim said.

6. "Lots and lots of books!" yelled Maria.

7. "H-m-m," said Mrs. Poppins. She wrote in her book what Maria said.

8. "I'd like a computer to check out books," said a voice in the back.

9. Mrs. Poppins looked up. She saw the librarian, Miss Page. "I think we can do that," Mrs. Poppins replied.

Page 101

Hello, Goodbye!

> A letter starts with **greeting** words (Dear) and ends with **closing** words (Love).
>
> *Dear Nancy,*
> *How was your trip?*
> *Love,*
> *John*

Write greetings, closings, and names on the line for each letter. Some suggestions are at the bottom of the page.

Answers will vary.

I miss you! I wish you would move back. Second grade isn't the same without you.

_____ ,
_____

Please come to my birthday party on Saturday.

_____ ,
_____

I tried your cereal. It was great. I got some at the store. Do you like yogurt?

_____ ,
_____

How are you? Will you be coming for the summer? Mom is so excited. Call us and tell us when your plane arrives.

_____ ,
_____

Greetings	Closings
Dear _____,	Love,
Hi _____,	Missing you,
Dear Sir,	Sincerely,
Hey friend,	

Page 102

Dear . . .

> When you write a letter, you must include certain things. You must have: a date, a greeting, a body, a closing, and a signature.
>
> greeting ⟶ *Dear Jane,*   April 21 ⟵ date
>   *I miss you!* ⟵ body
> closing ⟶ *Love,*
>   *Bob* ⟵ signature

On the form below, write a letter to a friend or family member. Remember to include all the elements of a letter.

_____
Answers will vary.
_____
_____
_____
_____
_____
_____
_____
_____
_____
_____
_____

Page 103